LIFE IN KIWI COUNTRY

by ROSEMARY HEPÖZDEN

WHITE CLOUD BOOKS

Canadian-born **Rosemary Hepözden** discovered her inner Kiwi when her nomadic father brought the family to settle in New Zealand in 1969. Despite frequent travels abroad, she always returns to Aotearoa, thanks to a deep and persistent conviction that there is nowhere better on earth. Rosemary Hepözden is also the author of *Instant Kiwi: New Zealand in a Nutshell*; *The Daily Male: A Kiwi Bloke's Book of Days*; and *Sorted: A Curious Kiwi Book of Lists*. She recently edited *Arohanui: My Aotearoa New Zealand*, published by Upstart Press in 2025.

A catalogue for this book is available from the National Library of New Zealand.

ISBN 978-1-77694-095-0

First Published in 2026 by
White Cloud Books
An imprint of Upstart Press Ltd
26 Greenpark Road
Penrose
Auckland 1061

Design Nick Turzynski, redinc. book design, www.redinc.co.nz

Printed by Everbest Printing Co. Ltd., China on paper sourced from sustainable forests

CONTENTS

FOREWORD

It was the end of a long day, and the delegates were thirsty. They had gathered in the hotel bar after the International Symposium on Small Secrets, where the secrets had stubbornly stayed unspilt. Someone — an American, we suspect — leaned across the bar and asked, "So, where on earth is New Zealand, anyway?"

"41° South, 174° East," snapped the cartographer.

"Opposite Salamanca, Spain," suggested the trivia buff.

"Across the Ditch," drawled the Australian.

"Twenty-seven hours from London," calculated the pilot.

"Between New Caledonia and Nicaragua, if you'd kindly check the catalogue," sighed the librarian.

The Proud Kiwi slammed his beer down.
"New Zealand is at the centre of the bloody universe, as far as we're concerned — and that's the way we like it."

Chapter One

WHERE ON EARTH IS NEW ZEALAND?

A Small Country Far from Everywhere

In truth, New Zealand is a long way from just about everything. It's a smallish country, usually found in the bottom right-hand corner of the map. There's a North Island, a South Island, and a smaller one called Stewart Island. Scattered beyond are some 600 other islands, most of them far-flung. The biggest of these other islands, the Chatham Islands, sit about 870 km (540 mi) southeast of the mainland — far enough to run on their own time zone.

If you stretched a tape measure down the country in a gentle curve from the northern tip of the North Island to the southernmost point on Stewart Island, the distance would be just over 1,600 km (1,000 mi). We have somewhere between 15,000 km and 18,000 km (9,824–11,185 mi) of coastline — nobody can be exactly sure, because it wriggles in and out of headlands and harbours, inlets and estuaries.

The Case of the Missing Country

If you're still squinting at the map, don't blame your geography skills. New Zealand has a peculiar habit of disappearing from world maps. Not metaphorically — literally.

We've been left off world maps by IKEA, Forbes, the BBC, the United Nations Office in Switzerland, Starbucks, the World Bank, the Smithsonian Institution in Washington, D.C., and the board games Pandemic and Risk. We were also missing from a British A-level geography textbook, Pyongyang's airport, Central Park Zoo and — perhaps most insultingly — from the official promotional material for the 2015 Rugby World Cup, despite the All

Blacks being reigning champions at the time.

By 2018, the omissions had piled so high that prime minister Jacinda Ardern teamed up with comedian Rhys Darby of Flight of the Conchords for a tongue-in-cheek campaign with an unequivocal hashtag: #GetNZontheMap. In the spoof video, Darby points the finger at possible conspirators: Australians (keen to steal our tourists), the English (keen to erase the All Blacks), and the French (threatened by our sauvignon blanc). Or maybe, he realised, cartographers simply thought we were a mistake ...

Later, the situation was resolved, when Sir Peter Jackson

produced a Middle-Earth map with New Zealand firmly in its rightful place.

Conspiracy or carelessness, one thing is clear: if you move here, you may never quite escape having to explain to old friends back home exactly where you've landed.

This example appears regularly on Reddit. It sometimes takes people a little time to see the joke.

Aotearoa: A Cloud on the Horizon

Listen carefully to the Māori version of our national anthem, and at the end of the first verse you will hear another name for New Zealand: Aotearoa.

Legend credits Hine-te-aparangi, wife of the great voyager Kupe, for the inspiration behind this name. As she and Kupe sailed across the South Pacific Ocean, she spotted a cloud on the horizon and called out "He ao! He ao!" ("A cloud! A cloud!") Kupe realised they were finally getting somewhere, because when you're at sea, a cloud often signals the presence of land.

The North Island — and eventually the whole of New Zealand — became known as Aotearoa. Not everybody

agrees on the exact meaning of the word, and affection for this name varies between iwi (Māori tribes), but the most popular interpretation is "long white cloud", referring to Kupe's discovery so long ago.

Where Did the Name "New Zealand" Come From?

The first European to sight New Zealand was the Dutch explorer Abel Tasman. He arrived in 1642 but decided not to go ashore after a bloody encounter with local Māori in Golden Bay (near the northern tip of the South Island). Perhaps it was in his haste to depart that he made a fundamental error. He assumed the land was part of an island in Argentina known as Staten Island, so he called us "Staten Land". (What a noob — though in fairness, GPS wouldn't be invented for another 330 years.)

Three years later, Dutch mapmakers corrected the error and renamed it "Nieuw Zeeland" after the Dutch province of Zeeland, which means "sea-land".

Nieuw Zeeland and New Zealand

When Captain James Cook arrived in 1769, he drew the first map showing the whole coast of both the North and South Islands. He added British names to places he visited and anglicised Nieuw Zeeland to "New Zealand", which was far easier for English speakers to read and spell.

Some of us, though, think it's a bit odd to be named after a province on the far side of the world. "Aotearoa" just seems more *us*.

Two hundred and fifty years later, the matter is still

not entirely settled. Even though many Kiwis use "New Zealand" and "Aotearoa" interchangeably, public approval for "Aotearoa" as our official name hasn't quite reached tipping point.

In fact, the use of "Aotearoa" can create a bit of a ruckus.

What's wrong with Aotearoa?

In 2021, Te Pāti Māori (a left-wing political party advocating for Māori rights) launched a petition to formally adopt "Aotearoa". Within two days, more than 50,000 people had signed it; by the middle of the following year, the total had topped 70,000 — enough to get Parliament's attention. The petition was duly presented, discussed — and then filed away.

AOTEAROA

Fast-forward to 2025, and the debate reignited, again in Parliament. Green MP Ricardo Menéndez March, originally from Mexico, used "Aotearoa" in a question. Winston Peters, leader of the New Zealand First party (and never one to miss a scrap), pounced. Why, he demanded, should someone who arrived in 2006 be allowed to "change this country's name without the referendum and sanction of the New Zealand people?" Ouch.

Speaker Gerry Brownlee coolly swatted the protest aside, pointing out that "Aotearoa" already appears on our passports and banknotes, and pretty much everything else short of our supermarket receipt. Peters was unswayed, announcing he would simply refuse to answer any question that included that word. In the end, nothing calamitous happened. We got distracted by other matters. Possibly, a crucial sports match came on.

Godzone: the divine favourite

We've also got a nickname for our country. Or we did. In the late 19th century, Irish-born poet Thomas Bracken recorded his love for his adopted homeland of New Zealand in a long and stirring poem called *God's Own Country*. His enthusiasm was clearly contagious, because Richard ("King Dick") Seddon, the prime minister of the time, frequently used the phrase in his speeches and correspondence. The last time he used it was in a telegram composed shipboard on 10 June 1906, just before he departed Australia for New Zealand: "JUST LEAVING FOR GOD'S OWN COUNTRY." Sadly, this turned out to be a case of famous last words, because Seddon died suddenly before he reached home.

Eventually, of course, some wit couldn't resist condensing "God's Own Country" to "Godzone", and for a while it became our nickname. You don't hear it so often these days. The Christian undertones don't sit comfortably. (In the 2023 Census, over 51% of New Zealanders stated they had no religion.) The historian Dr Hirini Kaa

(Ngāti Porou, Ngāti Kahungunu and Rongowhakaata), who is also an Anglican minister, explained that the decline in popularity of "Godzone" was due to the fact that it reflected a Pākehā perspective that failed to take into proper account the diverse New Zealand experience.

What Did You Say the Name Was?

In 2013, the New Zealand Geographic Board made a startling discovery: the names "North Island" and "South Island" had never been made official, despite two centuries of use. Even more baffling, the Māori names Te Ika a Māui ("the fish of Māui") and Te Waipounamu ("the waters of greenstone") had quietly vanished from maps after the 1950s.

What to do? The Geographic Board decided to canvass public opinion.

Well! Opinions varied a great deal. Some thought introducing alternatives would cause confusion. Others said those North and South names were "somewhat bloody obvious". Some said Māori names would be an enchanting tourist drawcard. Others described the New Zealand Geographic Board as "cultural zealots" and any move towards new names as political correctness of the worst kind.

In the end, in typically Kiwi fashion, we split the difference. On 17 October 2013, the Board formalised the English names and gave the Māori ones equal legal status. Problem solved.

How Did New Zealand Even Get Here?

Scientists say New Zealand broke off from the

supercontinent Gondwanaland about 85 million years ago, leaving the Tasman Sea to flood into the gap. It's a credible theory — but painfully slow-moving.

Māori have a much more action-packed legend. The details of this story vary according to who's telling it, but the punchline remains the same.

A Good Day's Fishing

Māui was the youngest of five brothers. As he grew, he had so many hair-raising adventures — acquiring fire, holding back the sun, that sort of thing — that his brothers felt a bit uneasy in his company, and they certainly didn't want him joining their fishing expedition. Māui, however, had other ideas.

One day, he hid in the hull of his brothers' canoe, clutching a hook he had fashioned from a fragment of his grandmother's jawbone. Soon his brothers set sail, unaware of the stowaway on board. Only when they were far out to sea did Māui emerge from his hiding place. He urged them to sail even farther, well out of sight of land. Once the brothers began fishing, the bottom of their canoe was quickly filled with the catch.

Then Māui decided his moment had arrived. When his brothers refused to give him any bait, he whacked himself on the nose to produce blood to smear on his magic hook. He threw the hook over the side of the canoe, chanting some powerful prayers as he did so.

Almost immediately, he snared something huge that struggled and lunged on the end of his line.

Māui was worried what the sea god Tangaroa would think about his huge catch and told his brothers that he would go and seek forgiveness from the gods for landing it. He warned his brothers to stay away from the fish until his return. But his brothers got tired of waiting and began cutting pieces off the fish. The fish started to raise its fins and thrash around in agony as its flesh was mutilated. Soon the sun rose, and as its heat blazed down, the fish solidified and became land, and the scars that Māui's brothers had carved into it became valleys and mountains. Te Ika a Māui (the fish of Māui) is what we now know as the North Island.

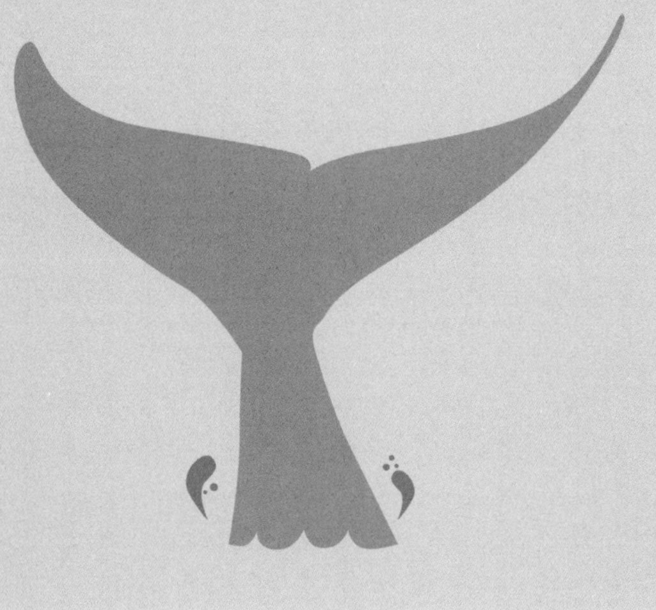

Time Travel

Distances from Auckland and approximate flight times:

City	Distance	Time
London	18,337 km / 11,394 mi	24 h 45 m
Istanbul	17,041 km / 10,589 mi	25 h 20 m
New York	14,194 km / 8,820 mi	16 h 15 m
New Delhi	12,530 km / 7,786 mi	16 h 20 m
Rio de Janeiro	12,268 km / 7,623 mi	23 h 30 m
Cape Town	11,763 km / 7,310 mi	17 h 35 m
Los Angeles	10,497 km / 6,523 mi	12 h 15 m
Shanghai	9,383 km / 5,830 mi	12 h 30 m
Hong Kong	9,140 km / 5,679 mi	11 h 30 m
Tokyo	8,840 km / 5,493 mi	10 h 55 m
Singapore	8,420 km / 5,233 mi	10 h 45 m
Manila	8,061 km / 5,010 mi	10 h 10 m

These flight times might tempt you to think New Zealand must surely be at the bottom of the world. Nope. The closest land to the South Pole is the southern tip of South America — so we can hardly be called the last place on earth.

Sizing Us Up

In moments of insecurity, we might compare ourselves to giants like China (35 × bigger) or Australia (28 × bigger) and question our significance.

But we're still much bigger than many places:

- 6.5 × bigger than Switzerland
- 245 × bigger than Hong Kong
- 381 × bigger than Singapore
- 45,089 × bigger than Gibraltar
- 113,928 × bigger than Monaco
- 541,068 × bigger than Vatican City

The easy way to think of it is this: we're a little bit bigger than the United Kingdom, and a bit smaller than Italy.

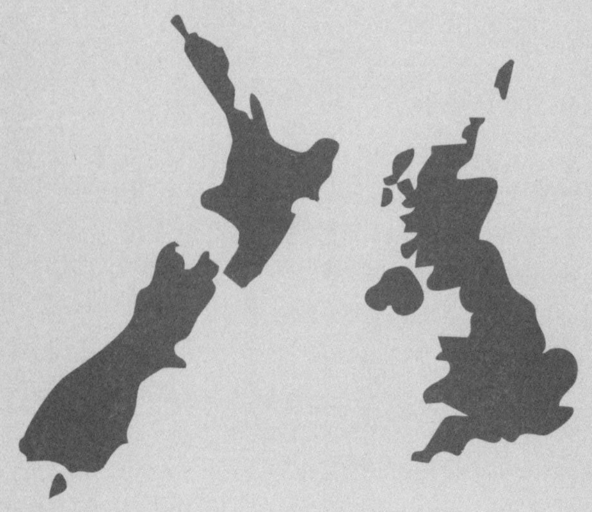

Placenames you won't find on the map

Across the Ditch — the "Ditch" is the Tasman Sea, so to go "across the Ditch" means to go to Australia

Down Under — a colloquial term for New Zealand (or Australia, or both)

West Island — a cheeky nickname for Australia

The Mainland — the South Island (used almost exclusively by South Islanders)

North Cape to the Bluff — from one end of New Zealand to the other

The Shaky Isles — New Zealand, nicknamed for our frequent earthquakes

HERITAGE MOMENT

The Country that Said "Yeah, Nah"

Back in 1901, when the six British colonies on the continent were preparing to unite as the Commonwealth of Australia, they sent an invitation across the Tasman Sea. New Zealand was welcome to become the seventh founding state. We politely declined. Many Kiwis still saw themselves as proudly British rather than Australasian, and the "twelve hundred miles of sea" between us felt insurmountable. (Besides, the Australians often dismissed us as "poor and backward cousins".) We stayed out, though from time to time, voices still wonder aloud whether we might have been better off joining after all.

Chapter Two

WILL THE REAL NEW ZEALAND PLEASE STAND UP?

For a small country, New Zealand has a surprisingly large reputation. You probably heard the stories — that we're clean and green, have sheep galore, that rugby is our religion, and hobbits scramble about in the hills. Or maybe the chat was a bit more critical, revolving around isolation, cost of living, or the uncomfortable closeness of relatives in such a small country. The truth is, we're more complicated, more nuanced, more amusing ... and, sadly, sometimes less picture-perfect than all of that.

Myth 1: We're clean and green

It's our brand. It's in the ads, the speeches, the tourist brochures: New Zealand, pure and pristine. The clean-and-green myth endures because it's almost true, and the postcards are irresistible. And to be fair, we do have scenery that makes jaws drop — fiords, volcanoes, beaches, rainforests. But "100% pure?"

Reality check:

- Many rivers and lakes are regularly unsafe for swimming, especially after rain.
- Agriculture is the largest source of our greenhouse gases, driven mostly by livestock methane.
- New Zealanders generate more municipal waste per person than the OECD average.
- Much of our original forest has been cleared for farming and forestry, leaving only fragments of native bush. A lot of native species are threatened, so "100% pure" is a brand, not a scientific claim.

Myth 2: There are no full-blooded Māori left

This debate crops up surprisingly often, and it can be offensive because it suggests that someone with "less than

100% Māori ancestry" is somehow less Māori. In te ao Māori, identity doesn't work that way. Being Māori is about whakapapa (genealogy), cultural connection, and belonging — not blood quantum.

Reality check:

- In Māori culture, any person with Māori ancestry who identifies as Māori is accepted as Māori.
- Whakapapa (genealogy) is the foundation of identity, not percentages of "blood".
- The very question of "full blood" reflects colonial thinking rather than Māori ways of defining identity.

Myth 3: We're still tied to Britain's apron strings

Once upon a time — even as recently as the 1970s — British immigrants were told that they'd find New Zealand just like their home country but lagging behind by 20 years. We drank endless cups of tea, celebrated the Queen's birthday, talked of the Motherland, and were steadfastly loyal. Young Kiwis' semi-obligatory OE ("Overseas Experience") involved a couple of years in London, usually working in a pub. But these days, tying ourselves to the Crown feels more anachronistic than automatic.

Reality check:

- Britain used to take over half of our exports. Now it accounts for only about 2%.
- The 2023 UK-NZ Free Trade Agreement didn't suddenly make the UK our biggest partner. Australia and China remain far more important.
- More Kiwis live in Australia (around 700,000) than in the UK.
- King's Birthday endures as a public holiday, not a plebiscite on loyalty.

- In a 2023 poll, fewer than half favoured keeping the monarchy; about a third said they would vote for a republic.

Myth 4: There are 20 sheep for every New Zealander

This was once true, and the image sufficiently entertaining that the myth endured. In 1982, sheep did outnumber us more than 20 to one. But since then, sheep numbers have shrunk while people numbers have climbed. Dairy, forestry, and urbanisation have changed the land-use mix, and the country that "lived off the sheep's back" now earns more from cows.

Reality check:

- New Zealand had about 23.6 million sheep in 2024. That's about 4½ per person, the lowest since the 1850s.
- Dairy cattle: about 4.7 million (2023–24) — a major land use.
- Lamb is not our most-consumed meat; chicken and beef are more affordable and therefore more popular.
- Sheep numbers still matter globally: New Zealand is the world's third-largest wool exporter (behind Australia and China).

Myth 5: Kiwis love the great outdoors

The brochures show trampers, kayakers, skiers, surfers, and mountain bikers — and many of us are. But not everyone is an adventurer. Money, time, health, and cultural disposition all shape who gets out and how often.

Reality check:

- Only about half of adults meet the 150-minutes-a-week activity guideline, and fewer than half visit natural areas each month.

- In 2021/22, only 45% of New Zealanders reported visiting a protected natural area in the previous month.
- Skiing holidays are out of reach for many Kiwis, when you consider transport, accommodation, shuttle and lift passes, equipment hire — and possibly a few lessons.
- Outdoor participation is broad but uneven; cost and access remain barriers.

Myth 6: New Zealand is safe and crime-free

Compared to many places, it is safer, but "crime-free" is a fantasy. Burglaries, scams, family violence, and road deaths are part of the picture.

Reality check:

- Safer than many places, yes — but family violence, burglaries, scams and road deaths are persistent issues.
- Family violence makes up a large share of serious harm and homicides.
- Cyber fraud costs New Zealanders millions each quarter.

Myth 7: We're a classless society

We like to think so: no aristocracy, no palaces . . .we're even on first-name terms with our prime minister. But economic reforms in the 1980s and 1990s and a cultural shift that took place with the influx of overseas media influence and consumer goods increased the gap between the richest and the poorest Kiwis. Inequality now shows up in housing, schooling, and wealth.

Reality check:

- The top 20% of households hold about 69% of net wealth.
- Pay gaps persist and are wider for Māori and Pacific women.

- Schooling is mostly public: about 85% state, about 11% state-integrated, about 4% private.

Myth 8: Gisborne is the first place in the world to see the sunrise

It's a proud East Coast boast: Gisborne, the first city to see the sun. Often true — especially for New Year's Day celebrations at East Cape or on Maunga Hikurangi, the first point on the New Zealand mainland to greet the dawn. But thanks to time-zone quirks, some Pacific islands beat us to it.

Reality check:

- Sorry, Gisborne — the Chathams always sneak in first, by 45 minutes.
- East Cape is the easternmost tip of the North Island, so it catches the sun before Gisborne city.
- Maunga Hikurangi (1,752 m) is the first *elevated* point on the mainland to see the sun.
- Kiribati's Line Islands (UTC+14) are even further ahead — they see the new day before New Zealand does.

Myth 9: There are no snakes in New Zealand

Not quite. Compared with Australia, we feel blissfully snake-free. Snakes are illegal to keep as pets, and they're treated as a top biosecurity risk. But that doesn't mean snakes never appear.

Reality check:

- Live snakes do get intercepted at the border. In August 2025, Biosecurity NZ intercepted a live wolf snake wrapped around a jandal in a suitcase arriving from Bali.
- Yellow-bellied sea snakes, highly venomous, sometimes wash ashore. Most strandings follow storms or unusual currents pushing them south.

- We have geckos and skinks instead, and none are found anywhere else in the world.

Myth 10: We're isolated from the rest of the world

"Nuclear-free and miles from anywhere" sounds like a recipe for purity and peace. Anytime global conflict breaks out, we wouldn't trade places with Europe (or anywhere else, for that matter) for anything. Yes, we are remote — no land borders, oceans on all sides. But isolation is a half-truth. In a digital world, we stream the same shows, buy the same brands, and doomscroll the same news as everyone else.

Reality check:

- You can fly from Auckland to New York City with no stopovers. (Yes, it's one of the world's longest direct flights, but at least on Air New Zealand the onboard wine selection will be good.)
- New Zealand is almost within spitting distance of Australia . . . a mere 2,100 km. In 1977, Colin Quincey — English-born, but we'll claim him — *rowed* across.
- Over 98% of New Zealanders use the internet daily.
- International tourists aren't deterred by our remoteness. In a post-Covid recovery, we've rebounded to receiving more than 3 million visitors a year.
- The Southern Cross undersea fibre-optic cables link us directly to Sydney, Los Angeles, and Asia.

Myth 11: The police don't carry guns

It's true that New Zealand police don't routinely carry sidearms on their belts. That sets us apart from many countries. But the idea that our police are "unarmed" is misleading; firearms are readily accessible and increasingly visible in certain situations.

Reality check:

- Frontline patrol cars carry secured firearms that officers can access when needed.
- Armed Offenders Squads operate nationwide; specialist units routinely carry firearms.
- Officers in airports, diplomatic protection, and specialist units do carry firearms routinely.

Myth 12: New Zealanders are all laid-back

The stereotype says Kiwis are relaxed, friendly, easygoing, and never in a hurry. It's true we value a "no worries, she'll be right" vibe, but stress, long hours, and financial pressure are just as real here as anywhere.

Reality check:

- Full-time workers put in an average of 42.7 hours a week.
- One in four New Zealanders report high levels of work stress.
- Household debt levels are among the highest in the developed world.
- Mental health services are stretched, with rising demand across all age groups.
- A lot of migrants feel that the "friendliness" is overplayed. It can take years before you get invited into a Kiwi home.

Myth 13: It's cheap to live here

Maybe it was, once upon a time, but it's no longer true for Kiwis. Eavesdrop in any supermarket, or even just turn on the radio, and you'll hear endless moaning about the cost of groceries and how everything is more expensive (and wages lower) here than in Australia. Food, housing, and fuel are often more expensive than people expect, thanks to import costs, limited competition, and high demand. There are ways to live cheaply — grow your own veg, shop at weekend markets, hunt out The Warehouse specials — but compared with many countries, the cost of living here is steep.

Reality check:

- By global measures, New Zealand is consistently among the more expensive places to live.
- The average household spends around $305 a week on food (about $15,800 a year).
- Petrol costs more than many OECD countries.
- In 2024 the Auckland City Mission distributed nearly 40,000 food parcels, while food hubs across the NZ Food Network supported more than half a million people each month.

Myth 14: DIY is in our DNA

Because New Zealand was small, remote, and short on imported goods, earlier generations learned to patch, mend, and invent. That history bred the "No. 8 wire" legend — the belief that every Kiwi can whip up a solution with whatever's at hand. (The phrase "No. 8 wire" comes from the fencing wire farmers used for endless improvisations.)

Reality check:

- DIY culture is strong, but not universal; lots of jobs still need licensed trades.
- Urban lifestyles, safety rules, and specialist skills mean Kiwi ingenuity doesn't always — or can't legally — stretch that far.
- ACC's "Have a hmmm" campaign exists for a reason: thousands of New Zealanders injure themselves each year attempting DIY and home maintenance.

Myth 15: New Zealand is not a racist country

We like to believe we're fair-minded and tolerant. Compared to some places, our multicultural mix does feel welcoming. But to say we're free of racism is wishful thinking. Inequities, prejudice, and discrimination still shape too many lives.

Reality check:

- The Human Rights Commission regularly receives thousands of complaints each year about racial discrimination.
- Māori and Pacific peoples face higher rates of unemployment and lower average incomes than Pākehā.
- A 2021 survey found nearly 40% of Asian New Zealanders reported experiencing discrimination.
- Hate crimes are under-reported, but spikes in racist abuse have followed global events (e.g. 9/11, the Christchurch mosque attacks).

Myth 16: Everyone knows everyone

In small towns, it might feel true. Neighbours recognise your car, shopkeepers remember your name, and news travels fast. But in the cities, especially Auckland, enjoying neighbourliness with the neighbours can be rare. The myth persists because with only five million people, it's easier to trace connections ("my cousin flatted with your brother"). But "everyone knows everyone" is more of a quip than a reality.

Reality check:

- New Zealand's total population (about 5.3 million) is smaller than many single world cities, but most of us live in urban areas where anonymity is common.
- Around 40% of settlements have fewer than 10,000 residents, which feeds the perception of intimacy. Yet the

majority of New Zealanders don't live in those towns.

- While 61% of people feel they belong in their neighbourhood, that leaves nearly four in ten who don't. Social connectedness is uneven.
- With almost 30% of residents born overseas, many Kiwis are building networks from scratch rather than relying on family webs of connection.

> *"The truth about New Zealand is that utopia doesn't exist . . . yet. But I'm happy to live here while we wait."*
>
> — OTIS FRIZZELL, ARTIST

Chapter Three
WHO ARE THE NEW ZEALANDERS?

The arrival of the Māori

Until about 800 years ago, Aotearoa was empty of human beings. Then, at about the same time as the Renaissance was stirring in Europe, the ancestors of today's Māori found their way to these shores.

These Polynesians were brilliant navigators who explored vast areas of the South Pacific Ocean in waka (canoes). They fixed their direction using the sun and stars, watched for cloud formations above unseen mountains, followed migrating birds, and even detected subtle shifts in wave patterns as vibrations through the hull of their vessels. Once they reached new land, they could sail back home to share the news and guide others back.

For a long time, people believed the "Great Fleet" story — that Māori arrived together in seven canoes — but archaeologists now think they came in several waves from around 1250-1300 onwards.

The arrival of the Europeans

Four hundred years passed before European explorers stumbled on New Zealand, and not all arrivals felt welcome.

Abel Tasman, sailing for the Dutch East India Company, sighted the mountains of the South Island on 13 December 1642. Days later, near Golden Bay (then named Murderers Bay), two waka paddled out to inspect his ships. The Māori blew long wooden trumpets to challenge the strangers; the Dutch replied with their own brass instruments, thinking it polite. It was anything but. The Māori took the blast as a sign of aggression. When Tasman's men tried to send a small boat across to greet them, a skirmish broke out, and four Dutch sailors were killed. Tasman never set foot on land. Shaken, he turned back and wrote that the inhabitants were hostile and contact would be dangerous. His grim report kept other Europeans away for decades.

James Cook had better luck. He reached New Zealand in 1769 aboard the *Endeavour*, charted the coastline with extraordinary accuracy, and on three separate voyages explored almost every inlet, headland and harbour. Although there were bloody encounters on his first visit, Cook came to describe Māori as having "a brave, noble, open and benevolent disposition." (On a later voyage, 10 of his men were killed and eaten at Grass Cove, though Cook wasn't there at the time.) His detailed maps and enthusiastic reports transformed New Zealand's reputation in European minds from hostile and savage to rich with promise.

Still, even fifty years later, barely a few hundred settlers had followed — mainly whalers, sealers, timber traders, flax dealers and earnest missionaries. Everyone else decided the distance was too great, the conditions too hard, and the rewards too few.

Waves of migration

Things changed with the signing of the Treaty of Waitangi in 1840. The New Zealand Company began selling hundred-acre lots in London and pitching a liberating new life. The dream was rosier than the reality: much of the land hadn't been properly purchased from Māori, and it needed heavy clearing before it could be farmed. Food was scarce, and the colony teetered on the brink of collapse.

In the 1860s, gold fever in the South Island brought a rush of Australians, Chinese, Americans, Scandinavians and

Europeans such as Dalmatians, Greeks and Italians. Chinese miners worked long days in icy rivers for a few grains of gold; many never made enough to return home. Dalmatian labourers dug for kauri gum in the swamps of Northland, living in rough bush camps.

The 1870s brought the most intense migration yet, spurred by British government schemes and starry-eyed promises of a "land of oil, olives and honey ... the promised land for you." By the mid-1870s, the non-Māori population was already over 250,000. The gold rushes had swelled the numbers, and though things slowed during the long depression of the 1880s, the growth never stopped. Assisted migration schemes, new farms, and the refrigerated shipping trade kept drawing people in. By 1950, the non-Māori population had climbed to around 1.9 million — a long way from the tiny handful of settlers just a century earlier.

In the 1950s, the New Zealand government offered financial incentives to boost the population. Out of some 400,000 new arrivals, more than 76,000 British and 20,000 Dutch came as assisted immigrants, the Dutch bringing their dairying skills (and decent coffee). The first Asian students arrived from Malaysia, Thailand and Indonesia, followed in the 1960s by 50,000 labourers from Samoa, the Cook Islands, Niue and Tokelau. These Pasifika communities reshaped suburbia, music, church life and rugby league.

The 1980s saw arrivals from Tonga and Indo-Fijian communities, alongside refugees from Laos, Cambodia and Vietnam. From 1987 onwards, a new points-based system attracted skilled migrants from such places as China and South Africa — planting everything from noodle shops to dumpling bars to night markets into our cities.

A population remix

According to the 2023 Stats NZ Census, Aotearoa has never been more diverse:

European/Pākehā 67.8%

Māori 17.8%

Asian 17.3%

Pacific Peoples 8.9%

MELAA (Middle Eastern, Latin American, African) 1.8%

(Totals exceed 100% because many people identify with more than one group.)

Nearly 29% of New Zealanders were born overseas, hailing from more than 200 countries. The "non-European" groups combined now make up almost a third of our population.

Who are the new New Zealanders?

In the 1950s, "New Zealander" meant more or less the same thing: over 85% of our foreign-born residents came from Australia or Great Britain.

Within three generations we went from "British backwater" to "vibrantly multicultural", and nowhere shows this shift more clearly than Auckland, where nearly 45% of residents were born overseas. On a single rush-hour bus you might hear Samoan, Mandarin, Tagalog, Hindi and te reo Māori in one breath. Diwali lights up Eden Park, Lunar New Year parades dance through the CBD, and Pacific church choirs belt out hymns on Sunday mornings. It's a city alive with different faces, languages, flavours and stories — and it offers a glimpse of where the whole country is headed.

All Present and Accounted For?

Kiwis love to travel. Some like it so much they never quite make it back.

By June 2023, there were about 700,000 New Zealand-born people living in Australia, making us their fourth-largest migrant group. Around 60,000 Kiwis live in Britain; 27,000 in the United States; and 15,000 in Canada. Add it up and you get well over 800,000 New Zealanders living overseas — proof that while we may call Aotearoa home, plenty prefer to keep their passports busy.

Now You Can Be a New Zealander

Until 2006, the Stats NZ census asked everyone to choose from five categories: European, Māori, Asian, Pacific or "Other". This created an identity conundrum. Why call yourself "European" if your family had been here for generations? And what if you were a bit of a mixture?

In the 2006 census, the rules changed: for the first time, people could identify simply as "New Zealander". We finally seemed to know who we were and were happy to say so.

Today, someone who's been here a year, cheers for the Black Ferns and complains about the price of butter, might feel just as Kiwi as someone whose ancestors signed the Treaty. What matters now is not just where you're from, but where you call home.

Kiwi by heritage

Australians must feel a bit hard done by. It's bad enough that they're attempting to lure so many of our nurses and police officers, but what else could be behind their brazen attempts to claim some of our local legends? A few of the many they've attempted to poach:

- Nancy Wake — fearless WWII spy nicknamed "the White Mouse" (born in Wellington, 1912)
- Phar Lap — champion racehorse (foaled in Timaru in 1926)
- Keith Urban — Grammy-winning country singer (born in Whangārei)
- Split Enz — formed by Te Awamutu lads Tim and Neil Finn (they added the "z" to assert their Kiwi roots)
- Russell Crowe — born in Wellington, schooled at Auckland Grammar School, and forever one of ours.

Kiwi at heart

To be fair, we've done a bit of people-poaching too. A few who weren't born here but who we proudly consider Kiwis:

- Beatrice Tinsley — astronomer, born in England
- Derek Handley — entrepreneur, born in Hong Kong
- Eleanor Catton — author, born in Canada
- Anna Paquin — born in Winnipeg, Canada, raised in NZ, youngest-ever Academy Award winner
- Irene van Dyk — netball great, born in South Africa
- Jane Hunter — pioneering winemaker, born in South Australia
- Keisha Castle-Hughes — actor, born in Western Australia
- Lydia Ko — golfing prodigy, born in South Korea
- Oscar Kightley — writer and comedian, born in Samoa
- Sam Neill — actor, born in Northern Ireland

The New Kiwi Roll Call

Once it was coast-to-coast Smiths, Browns, Williamses and Joneses. Now the names in the birth notices are reshaping what "Kiwi" looks like. In 2024, the most common surname for babies born in New Zealand was Singh, reflecting our fast-growing Sikh community (53,000 strong at the last Census).

A trans-Tasman truth

An oldie but a goodie came from former Prime Minister Rob Muldoon. In the 1980s, when asked about the steady stream of Kiwis moving to Australia, he quipped that anyone who left New Zealand for Australia was raising the average IQ of both countries. (He pinched the joke from Will Rogers, but we didn't mind. Anything that puts us in a favourable light is funny.)

HERITAGE MOMENT

Who owns the pavlova?

Australians like to say a Perth chef invented the pavlova in the 1930s. Nice try ... but New Zealand had it on the table first. The *Oxford English Dictionary* traces the earliest pavlova recipe to New Zealand in 1927 (just quietly, it had a jelly base — but we'll let that slide). By 1928–29, Kiwi cookbooks were already serving up the true meringue version. Food historian Professor Helen Leach later uncovered 21 New Zealand recipes in print before 1940, years before the first Australian examples. The verdict? Pavlova belongs to us. Sorry, Aussies — stick to your lamingtons.

Chapter Four

MĀORI: THE KIWI FIRSTS

When Captain James Cook arrived in 1769, about 100,000 Māori were already here. Today, according to the 2023 Census, 887,493 people identify as Māori (about 18% of New Zealanders), and about one in five are of Māori descent (978,246).

What does "Māori" mean?

In te reo, "māori" began as an adjective meaning "ordinary, natural, local". You still hear it in "wai māori" (meaning "freshwater"). Before Europeans arrived, the word wasn't used as a blanket term for the indigenous people because there was no need for one; there were no separate races to differentiate. After contact, it became the collective term distinguishing tangata whenua (people of the land) from Pākehā, and it was in common use by the 1830s.

What does being Māori mean?

In the Māori worldview, being Māori is about whakapapa (genealogy) — your links to your ancestors, your land and your iwi/hapū (tribe). It has nothing to do with "how much Māori blood" you've got; there isn't a checklist or a sliding scale that determines how Māori you are. The old talk of fractions ("full-blood", "three-quarters", and so on) belongs in the past.

Pepeha: saying who you stand with

That's why a pepeha matters. It's a short introduction that places you in relation to land and people: your maunga (mountain), awa (river), waka (ancestral canoe), iwi and hapū, often your marae — and then you. You'll hear pepeha at the start of pōwhiri (traditional welcoming ceremonies) and hui (meetings), and increasingly in workplaces and classrooms, too. It explains not just who you are, but who you stand with.

So what does Pākehā mean, then?

Pākehā is a Māori word widely used for New Zealanders of European descent. Its exact origin is uncertain, but it was in use before 1815 and wasn't originally derogatory. In official stats, the census wording is "European/New Zealand European", though many people are happy to self-describe simply as Pākehā.

The Treaty of Waitangi: Where the trouble began

The Treaty of Waitangi (Te Tiriti o Waitangi) was signed on 6 February 1840 by the British Crown's representative and a large number of Māori chiefs. Further signings followed around the country on multiple sheets. In total, more than 500 chiefs signed.

The Treaty consisted of three articles. In brief:

- The Crown would govern New Zealand.
- Māori would keep authority over their lands, villages and treasured things; if land was sold, it would be offered to the Crown first.
- Māori would have the same rights and protections as British people.

And we thought it was going so well

But there was a problem: there were two versions of the Treaty — one in English and one in Māori — and they are not exact translations of each other. The different interpretations have led to nearly two centuries of confusion, conflict, and legal debate.

In the years after the Treaty of Waitangi was signed, the government took Māori land through unfair laws and wars. Between the signing of the Treaty and 1950, Māori landholdings shrank from almost all of Aotearoa to about five percent of the country's land area.

But for Māori, land ownership is not just about possession. It is about a deep spiritual connection to their ancestors and culture. Land represents well-being, cultural identity, and a key to economic independence. When left without enough land to farm or live on, many Māori drifted to urban centres, settling in poorer areas, where bias was common across education, health care, housing and employment.

Stick to your promises

Toitū te Tiriti means "Uphold the Treaty". It's a contemporary movement calling for Aotearoa to honour the Māori version of Te Tiriti o Waitangi. Supporters believe the promises made in the Māori text — especially tino rangatiratanga (self-determination) — have never been properly upheld. They point to ongoing inequities in housing, health, education, and justice as signs the Treaty has been sidelined rather than respected. The movement sees Te Tiriti as a living agreement that should guide decisions today.

You'll see "Toitū te Tiriti" on placards, on T-shirts, at protests, in social media hashtags, and in public debate. It's a call to honour the deal that was signed.

The marae: standing on sacred ground

A marae is a Māori communal facility with a meeting house, dining hall and cooking area. It symbolises the iwi (tribe) to whom it belongs. Although marae are communal, they are anything but a casual drop-in centre: all manuhiri (visitors) must be invited by a member of the tangata whenua (the owners of the marae). Before you go, it is worth learning about the tikanga (correct procedure) of being on a marae.

You're welcome: How to do a hongi

If you visit a marae and one of your Māori hosts leans towards you, you are being asked to share in a hongi, which is the traditional Māori greeting. Lean forward slightly, close your eyes, and let your forehead press lightly against theirs. Whether you press once or twice doesn't matter — the meaning is the same — but linger for about two seconds. You are sharing the breath of life, and your welcome to the marae is complete.

Saving a national treasure

Two hundred years ago, you would have heard more Māori language (te reo Māori) spoken in this country than English. With the arrival of more and more settlers, however, the dominance of the Māori language diminished. Back then, te reo wasn't appreciated as an essential tool for preserving culture, and its use in schools was actively discouraged. By the middle of the 20th century, te reo Māori was badly in need of maintenance; unless strenuous efforts were put into protecting and revitalising it, the Māori language would die out.

In 1985, the Waitangi Tribunal declared that the Māori language was a taonga (treasure) that the government had a duty to protect under the Treaty of Waitangi. On 1 August 1987, by Act of Parliament, te reo Māori became an official language of New Zealand.

Despite growing visibility of te reo Māori in public life, the proportion of Māori who say they can hold a conversation about a lot of everyday things in the language has actually fallen, from 26.1% in 2006 to just 18.4% in the 2023 Census. For the total population, it sits at 4.3%. While revitalisation efforts are having an impact, conversational fluency remains a major challenge, especially beyond the classroom or the marae. Exposure to signage, greetings, and waiata helps, but doesn't always lead to confident speaking.

Still, hope lives in schools, on Māori Television, in kōhanga reo (language nests), kura kaupapa (Māori immersion schools), and whānau determined to reclaim the reo.

How do you say that?

Ngāruawāhia, pīpīwharauroa, pōhutukawa, pounamu, Whakarewarewa . . . In New Zealand, many of our placenames, as well as the names of birds, animals and trees, are Māori in origin, so it's worth learning a little about pronunciation.

1. **Every vowel is pronounced**
   There are 5 vowels: *a, e, i, o, u* — each has a clear, consistent sound.
2. **Macrons matter**
   A line over a vowel (like ā) means it's held longer: Māori vs Maori.
3. **"Wh" sounds like "f"**
   For example, whānau is pronounced like fah-no.
4. **"Ng" sounds like in "singer"**
   Not like in finger. Example: Whanganui = Fah-nga-noo-ee.

5. **No "s" for plurals**
   Tamariki means children. There's no tamarikis!

Modern Māori: te reo evolves

Just like other world languages, te reo Māori has to create new words to keep up with modern concepts, activities and technologies. The Māori Language Commission is the official source of new Māori equivalents of English words. If you want the word for "pizza", for example, or maybe "ping-pong" or "defensive driving", the commission will do an exhaustive search to check that the Māori equivalent doesn't already exist. If it doesn't, the Commission's scholars will coin a new word that retains the cultural integrity of te reo. The new word will be peer-reviewed before it and its derivation are entered into an electronic database of neologisms.

The Māori word for "pizza", by the way, is parehe, which means "flat cake of fern root".

The word for "ping-pong" is poikōpiko — from "poi" (meaning "ball"), and "kōpiko" (meaning "go alternately in opposite directions").

The Māori equivalent for "defensive driving" is karo aituā waka, from "karo" (meaning "avoid"), "aituā" (meaning "misfortune, trouble, disaster, accident"), and "waka" (meaning "vehicle").

Social media platforms such as X (formerly Twitter) have spawned many new words. The word tīhau, which means "the chirp of a bird", was selected as the equivalent of "tweet", and the word paetīhau was the obvious equivalent for "Twitter": "the perch or platform from where a bird tweets".

The essence of understanding

While you're getting to grips with te reo Māori, listen out for some much-respected abstract concepts. It's not always possible to find an exact translation:

aroha — love, compassion
iwi — a tribe or kinship group
kaitiakitanga — guardianship of the environment and its resources
koha — a contribution or donation, often given voluntarily
mana — prestige or status
manaakitanga — caring for the needs of others and showing kindness
mauri — the life force, metaphysical essence or energy
rāhui — temporary restrictions on accessing an area or a resource
rangatiratanga — self-determination; autonomy
taonga — a treasure or something deeply valued (not always a physical object)
te ao Māori — the Māori worldview
tikanga — customs and protocols; the right way of doing things
whakapapa — genealogy, lineage or descent
whānau — extended family, or a close-knit group like a community or team
whanaungatanga — building relationships and making connections

These words will pop up in invitations, meetings, political debates, and news stories — and you're expected to have a basic understanding of them.

Te Wiki o te Reo Māori (Māori Language Week)

Every September, Aotearoa makes a deliberate fuss about te reo Māori. Schools, councils, newsreaders, cafés, Shortland Street… everyone lifts their reo for a week. It began after a 1972 petition calling for Māori language in schools; by the mid-1970s it was a full week, and today it's shepherded nationally by Te Taura Whiri i te Reo Māori (the Māori Language Commission). The spirit is simple: make the language visible, audible, and normal.

Whittaker's "Miraka Kirīmi" moment

In 2022, Whittaker's gave one of their classic products a makeover for Māori Language Week. Their creamy milk chocolate bar became Miraka Kirīmi (literally "creamy milk"). A storm brewed online, starting with a grumble from the "too much te reo" crowd. "I support people learning te reo," one said, "but not in this manner. It feels like forced mandated injections." Others pushed back. "And I guess lots of folk will also be giving up pinot gris, champagne, savignon [sic] blanc, tacos, sushi, lasagne, spaghetti bolognaise, wontons, and pretty much any curry ever because they aren't in English either," one wrote.

Whittaker's brought the bar back the next year in larger numbers.

Moko kauae — a proud ID

Moko kauae is the traditional marking worn by Māori women. The practice of tattooing the chin faded during the 19th and early 20th centuries under colonisation and changing social pressures, but knowledge survived through kuia who had their moko in the 1920s–30s, and in recent decades there's been a powerful revival.

For many wāhine Māori, a moko kauae is not decoration but an outward sign of whakapapa and mana wāhine. You may hear it described like this: every Māori woman carries a moko within; when she's ready, the artist brings it to the surface.

Public visibility has grown with high-profile wāhine choosing moko kauae. In 2016 Nanaia Mahuta became the first woman in New Zealand's Parliament to wear one; in 2020 she became Foreign Affairs Minister, and media coverage often noted her kauae as a statement of identity. In 2021, broadcaster Oriini Kaipara became the first person with traditional facial markings to anchor a national prime-time news bulletin. These moments didn't invent the practice, but they helped normalise it.

Tā moko as an art has its own tikanga (protocol). Designs

are bespoke to the wearer and tell a story of ancestry and place. Many artists and whānau frame the decision to take a kauae as a milestone reached through kōrero, consent and readiness, not fashion. (Tā moko artist Julie Paama-Pengelly speaks of moko as "activating our desire to be proud of who we are".)

The simplest etiquette is this: admire, don't imitate, don't denigrate; each kauae belongs to the person who wears it. The resurgence you'll see on streets, screens and marae is part of a broader culture renaissance, guided by the people it belongs to.

Leading statements

- Tinirau, a great chief of the Whanganui district long ago, is quoted as saying "Toi tu te kupu, toi tu te mana, toi tu te whenua". He was saying that there were three essential ways of preserving Māoritanga: Māori language, honour, and land. Without them, Māori culture would be a thing of the past.
- In 2025, the new Māori Queen, Nga wai hono i te po Paki, spoke to her people for the first time since being crowned. "Being Māori is not defined by having an enemy or a challenge to overcome. Being Māori is speaking our language. It is taking care of the environment. It is reading and learning about our history. It is the choice to be called by our Māori name. There are many ways to manifest being Māori, not just in times of protest," she said.

HERITAGE MOMENT

Whale music for the Kauri

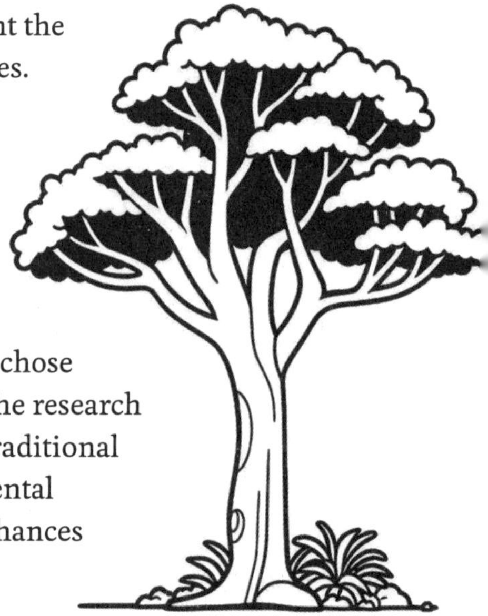

In 2024, environmental researchers tried an unusual way to fight the disease killing off kauri trees. Traditional Māori wisdom holds that kauri and whales are brothers — both descended from the god of the forest, Tāne Mahuta — but they were separated when the whales chose the ocean over the forest. The research team decided to combine traditional knowledge with environmental science to boost the trees' chances of recovery. They created a sound recording blending whale song, traditional Māori instruments, and karakia (blessings), and played it in the forest to the affected trees.

While critics questioned the $4 million cost, proponents valued it as a culturally meaningful and justifiable integration of traditional and modern science. Taxpayers' Union spokesman Jordan Williams said, "At $4 million, the very least taxpayers could expect is a copy of the CD."

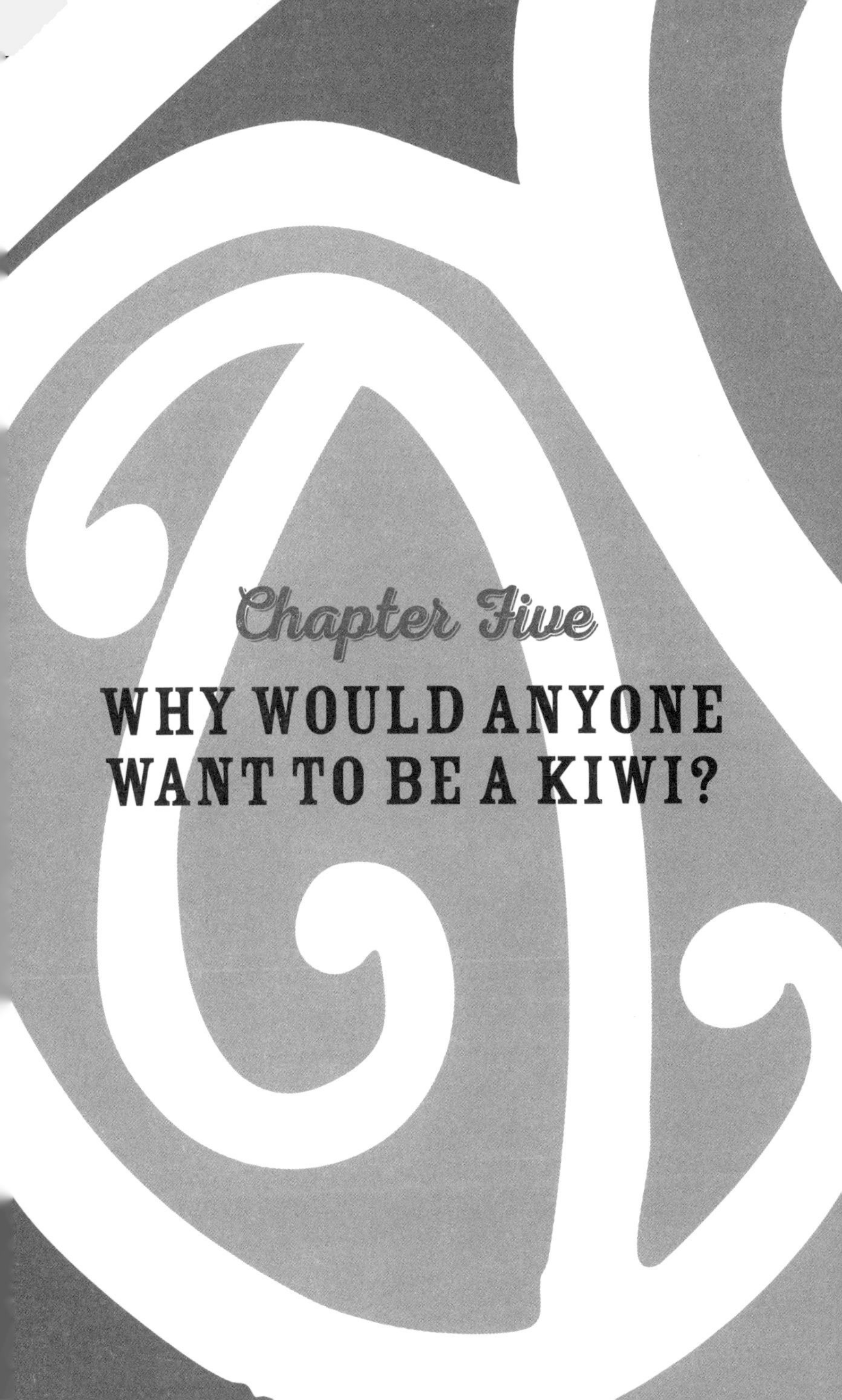

Chapter Five

WHY WOULD ANYONE WANT TO BE A KIWI?

In 2024, 43,586 people became New Zealand citizens. They came from all over — India, the UK, South Africa, the Philippines, Samoa, China, Fiji, Tonga, Germany, the United States — and *signed up to be Kiwis*. They chose to ignore the earthquakes and four seasons in one day, job scarcity and the hospital waiting lists, because a small country at the bottom of the map just sounded *better*. Actually, if you watch the nightly TV news, New Zealand can sound like a country in crisis. So why? Why on earth would anyone come here?

20 Very Good Reasons

- We've got elbow room. With only about 19 people per square kilometre, New Zealanders enjoy wide open spaces compared with the UK's 282 people per square kilometre (even though we're similar in area).
- We've got no real problems with the neighbours. They can be annoying if they beat us at sport, but we know that we'd have each other's backs if anyone threatened either one of us militarily. The ANZAC spirit still stands.
- Corruption is rare. Bribery isn't part of life here. The 2024 Corruptions Perceptions Index (published in 2025) ranked us at number 4 in the world — ahead of countries like Switzerland, Iceland and Canada.
- Paradise is close. When you need a quick top-up of sunshine, dream holiday destinations like Fiji, Samoa and the Cook Islands are practically around the corner — well, at least no more than a short flight north.
- We're not big on status. You don't have to struggle trying to be fancy. Yes, social inequalities exist, but most people are on a first-name basis, whether you're talking to the prime minister or your surgeon.

- The government is prohibited from imposing a state religion. Kiwis are guaranteed freedom of thought, conscience and belief, thanks to the NZ Bill of Rights Act 1990.
- You can stand out. In a smaller country, it's easier to make your mark. Peter Jackson said it: "One of the best things about growing up in New Zealand is that if you are prepared to work hard and have faith in yourself, truly anything is possible."
- Though violent, ugly rioting does break out sporadically, nobody dies. Our political dramas are tame compared with those in many countries. We don't invade other countries. In the 2025 Global Peace Index, we came third, just behind Iceland and Ireland.
- We're free to roam. A New Zealand passport opens the door to 185 countries without a visa or with visa-on-arrival. It's a great launchpad for exploring the world.
- The food is fresh. With much of it grown or caught locally, even supermarket produce can taste like it came from a farmers' market. And the wineries produce vintages of spectacular quality.
- Voting is optional (even if enrolling is not). And there's more than one party to choose from. You can engage — or not — without penalty. Civic freedom is a given.
- Healthcare is (mostly) free, though you might have to join a dishearteningly long waiting list for elective surgery. Hospital visits don't bankrupt you. GPs are subsidised, and kids under 14 get free visits to the doctor.
- Schooling is (mostly) free. Primary and secondary education is free in state schools, though "donations" are "suggested", and you'd have to have a very staunch constitution to resist the pressure to hand over the dollars.

- We've got plenty of tourist-worthy attractions — places to go, things to do, people to see — but we're not *swamped* by tourists. In 2023, New Zealand hosted roughly 6 overseas visitors per 10 residents. Imagine how the Greeks feel about that. In 2024, their country hosted about 40 tourists per 10 residents.
- Your spare room is probably safe. Free-loading house guests may be few and far between. Distance protects us because those long-haul flights are expensive. Relatives overseas will be content with a Zoom call instead.
- Nature is on your doorstep. Magnificent beaches, mountains, lakes, and rivers are usually within a couple of hours' drive, and there are no native land snakes to accidentally stand on.
- Military service is voluntary. There is no conscription. There are no child soldiers. You have to be at least 17 before you can join the Navy, the Army, or the Air Force (and only if you have your parents' consent).
- Sea views are normal. The farthest point from the coast is only 119km away. Coastal views are part of everyday life.
- We don't sue at the drop of a hat. Thanks to ACC, Kiwis are covered for most accidents — without the legal drama and exorbitant medical costs.
- Christmas really is better in summer, when you don't have to shovel snow from your front door and burden your digestive system with hot, rich, heavy food. A beach barbie and a cool dip in the sea does nicely.

In 2023, the General Social Survey produced a pass grade for Kiwi life. A few indicators were disappointing: trust in other people, trust in institutions and a sense of safety had eroded slightly over the previous two years. But only very slightly.

Overall, 77% of New Zealanders were satisfied with life.

Even so, Kiwis can become despondent quite easily. Global events — no matter how far away — make it hard to relax. Sometimes, all it takes is a defeat of the All Blacks to skewer the national mood. Take the historic victory of South Africa's Springboks in September 2025. The All Blacks lost by an embarrassing margin (43 — 10, if you really need to know), and within 24 hours, a pall of defeatism hung over the nation at large. Gregor Paul, an astute observer of the game, took the occasion to decry New Zealand as a whole. The Test was just another symptom, he said, of our whole nation going to the dogs. We had been duped in the past by an over-confident mindset, he said, and we ought to realise: "Rugby is just one more part of New Zealand in decline, one more thing eroding while everyone deludes themselves otherwise."

Kiwis' current woes

Pushed to explain what's keeping them awake at night, Kiwis would tell you these are their main concerns:

- Cost of living/inflation: Over 55% of Kiwis identify inflation and the rising cost of living as their top concern
- Healthcare/public health system: Hospitals report ED overcrowding and delayed access to specialists — and, in exceptional and extremely rare cases, patients dying in hospital corridors while waiting for a doctor to see them.
- Economy and job security: Roughly 47% are worried about their job security.
- Housing and homelessness: Rising rents threaten affordability and fuel homelessness.
- Poverty, inequality and welfare pressure: Welfare reliance

has surged — 400,000 people (the highest since the 1990s) — with food insecurity and homelessness on the rise.

- Public sector cuts and underfunding: Over 9,500 public sector jobs have been cut since 2023, impacting services like education, conservation, and health.
- Rising national debt and low growth: Debt is forecast to reach 45% of GDP by 2029.
- Emigration: In 2024–25, a record 69,100 citizens left NZ, potentially hollowing out the workforce; this is compounded by slower skilled immigration, fueling labour shortages in key regions.

"We don't know how propitious are the circumstances"

In 1975, John Clarke (aka Fred Dagg) recorded a song that soon became our unofficial national anthem, "We Don't Know How Lucky We Are". We needed to alter our perspective and perk up a bit, he sang. We agreed. The song reached number 17 on the New Zealand Music Charts.

Sounds like we should listen to it again.

You can call yourself Kiwi when . . . A +64 checklist

1. You know that's our international dialling code.
2. You've been to the dairy in bare feet.
3. You've played beach cricket with a chilly bin as the wicket.
4. Instead of complaining, you just get on with it.
5. You know what season a flowering pohutukawa heralds.

6. You've crossed the Cook Strait on a bad day.
7. You pronounce *Taupō* and *Whanganui* properly without thinking about it.
8. You know when the Bluff oyster season starts.
9. You're sad they can't save the Chateau Tongariro.
10. Matariki makes perfect sense; King's Birthday, not so much.
11. You've been to a marae and shared a hongi.
12. You always keep an eye out for your mates.
13. At some point, you've (unadvisedly) tried performing a haka.
14. You include a battered mussel or two in your order of fish and chips.
15. When you're truly grateful, you say "Thanks heaps."
16. You can easily identify the Southern Cross in the night sky.
17. You recognise that Kiwi culture changes "south of the Bombay Hills".
18. You know where everyone gets a bargain.
19. You've remarked at least once that New Zealand punches above its weight.
20. You know that "your shout" means you're paying.
21. You'd immediately recognise Sam Hunt if you saw him in the street.
22. You avoid Queenstown because it's too touristy.
23. You still haven't seen a kiwi in the wild.
24. You've shared your opinion on David Seymour.
25. You stash your pineapple lumps in the freezer.
26. You've slowed down to let a flock of sheep across the road.
27. You know that Russell Crowe was born in New Zealand.
28. You wonder when the rebuild of the Christchurch Cathedral will ever be complete.

29. You appreciate the qualities of an excellent sausage roll.
30. You support any team that beats the Aussies.
31. You love Peter Jackson even more for backing the project to “de-extinct” the giant moa.
32. You’re sick of sheep-shagger jokes.
33. You’ll never forget how offensive the bombing of the *Rainbow Warrior* was.
34. Somewhere in the back of your cupboard lurks a paua ashtray.
35. You’re ambivalent about the monarchy’s relevance to 21st century New Zealand.
36. You know which town was the first to greet the new millennium.
37. You care enough to disinfect your shoes whenever you enter or leave a kauri forest.
38. You’ve almost given up hoping Christmas Day will be sunny for once.
39. You know the score from the last All Blacks test.
40. You know what slip, slop, slap means — and you do it.
41. You were surprised that even now English is only a *de facto* official language of New Zealand.
42. You complain that “all the good fish gets exported”.
43. You instinctively take your shoes off at someone’s place (or ask if you should).
44. You’ve got strong feelings about feijoas, one way or another.
45. You recognise *Country Calendar*’s theme tune in the first few notes.
46. You can understand the outstanding beauty in a pair of Red Bands.
47. You sometimes hop over to Sydney or Melbourne for the weekend.

48. You know that Ninety Mile Beach isn't anything of the sort.
49. If there's no beetroot or fried egg in your burger, you sense that something's missing.
50. You get out of bed in time to attend an ANZAC Day Dawn Parade.
51. You find yourself standing next to your MP in the supermarket check-out lane.
52. You've thought about bungy-jumping but probably decided "Yeah, nah."
53. Your first response to a problem is "Right, let's give it a crack."
54. You own at least one piece of merino clothing.
55. In a cricket match, you would never, *ever* bowl underarm.
56. You know that it's a bach in the North Island and a crib in the South.
57. You know I can't grab your ghost chips.
58. You know that doing a bomb off a diving board is a "manu", and there's a "world championship" in Auckland every year.
59. You're devastated *Shortland Street* doesn't screen five nights a week.
60. When you travel overseas, you put a sticker of the New Zealand flag on your backpack.
61. You're embarrassed you haven't quite nailed the first verse of the national anthem, and you make up for it by singing the second verse much louder.
62. You frequently wonder whether you should pack up and move to Australia.
63. After weighing everything up, you decide life's better on this side of the ditch.
64. You can handle the jandal.

How "Kiwi" became our cultural ID

Before the 20th century, the kiwi was just one of various symbols used on banknotes, postage stamps and army badges, or in cartoons, to represent New Zealand. It took the loving tribute of an Australian to popularise the term to describe New Zealanders. In 1906, William Ramsay invented a shoe polish and decided to name it after the kiwi in honour of his wife's birthplace. Kiwi Shoe Polish was sold in the UK and the US during World War I and was widely used by soldiers to keep their boots clean and shiny.

It was only a small shift for the Allied soldiers to apply the name of their boot polish to their comrades from New Zealand. Perhaps the New Zealand soldiers were proud to be associated with such an idiosyncratic creature. In any case, the soldiers who occupied Sling Camp on Salisbury Plain in England during World War I carved a giant kiwi on the chalk hill above their wooden huts. Before long, New Zealand soldiers were widely known as "Kiwis".

In World War II, New Zealand soldiers again got the "Kiwi" nickname — and it not only stuck, it spread. It came to describe any New Zealander, not just soldiers. We didn't mind. Because the kiwi is the only bird of its kind, we decided it suited us rather well.

HERITAGE MOMENT

You do love us, don't you?

New Zealanders are sometimes uncomfortably proud of our country. That truth was nailed in 2007 when the Automobile Association published *I Love You New Zealand: 101 Must-Do's for Kiwis*. The opening line admitted what we often try to hide: "Parochialism is a Kiwi staple and our level of insecurity with regard to international visitors' opinions of New Zealand can be almost embarrassing." It captured perfectly the way Kiwis lean in when we meet newcomers: "So, what do you think of New Zealand? Oh, you haven't even left the airport yet? Well, what do you think of it anyway?"

A Kiwi Countdown: Numbers that add up to New Zealand

0 Trees left at the summit of One Tree Hill after Māori activist Mike Smith borrowed a mate's chainsaw and attacked the lone Monterey pine in 1994. It had stood there for 120 years. The protest was against the way Treaty of Waitangi negotiations were progressing.

1 The number of times a live moa has been spotted since the birds were declared extinct over 500 years ago. In 1993, Irish publican Paddy Freaney swore he'd seen "this bloody huge bird . . ." He even produced a photo, but the Department of Conservation decided it might have been a deer.

2 National anthems: "God Defend New Zealand" and "God Save the King". Which one we sing depends on whether any UK royalty are present.

3 Natural features that have been granted the same legal status as an individual person: Te Urewera, the Whanganui River, and Mount Taranaki. These landscapes are regarded as ancestors by the people who live nearby.

4 The number of stars on the New Zealand flag representing the Southern Cross — one fewer than the Australians feature on theirs.

5 Recognised species of kiwi (the bird), many still struggling for survival. Only about 5% of kiwi chicks in the wild survive into adulthood without human help.

6 New Zealand cities with 100,000+ people: Auckland, Christchurch, Wellington, Hamilton, Tauranga, and Dunedin.

7 Points scored by France in the 2011 Rugby World Cup final, one fewer than the 8 the All Blacks scored — giving New Zealand the Webb Ellis Cup in a nail-biter at Eden Park.

8 The gauge of the wire ("Number 8 wire") which became a Kiwi symbol of DIY ingenuity because it could be bent, twisted, or repurposed to fix just about anything.

9 Sacks of pipis among the haul my true love gave to me, according to "A Pukeko in a Ponga Tree" (our local take on the "Twelve Days of Christmas").

10 The $10 banknote features Kate Sheppard, leader of the New Zealand women's suffrage movement.

11 Nationwide public holidays each year. The most recent addition is Matariki (Māori New Year), a time for remembering, celebrating, and looking ahead with new hope.

12 The number of hardy souls in the scientific team wintering over each year at Scott Base, Antarctica. Numbers swell to around 85 in summer.

13 Issues of the *Australian Women's Weekly* (NZ Edition) published each year. It remains a staple of doctors' waiting rooms, WOF workshops, and hair salons.

14 Where our pension system ranks globally, according to a 2024 Mercer Index that assessed 48 systems. We scored a B: solid basics, but too many Kiwis tip only the bare minimum into KiwiSaver, and plenty aren't in it at all.

15 The average number of meat pies a Kiwi eats in a year.

16 The age at which you can get married or enter a civil union, as long as your parents say it's okay.

17 How old Lorde was when she won a Grammy for her song "Royals" in 2014.

18 The page in *Arohanui: My Aotearoa New Zealand* (2025, Upstart Press) where Sir Ashley Bloomfield reflects on our Covid response: "We showed kindness . . . We demonstrated that we care for each other, and this is still a point of difference from many other countries."

19 The Warriors' permanently retired jersey number, in honour of Sir Peter "the Mad Butcher" Leitch, one of their most ardent supporters.

20 The number of times a day Rotorua's Pōhutu Geyser, the largest geyser in the Southern Hemisphere, can erupt, blasting water and steam up to 30 metres into the air.

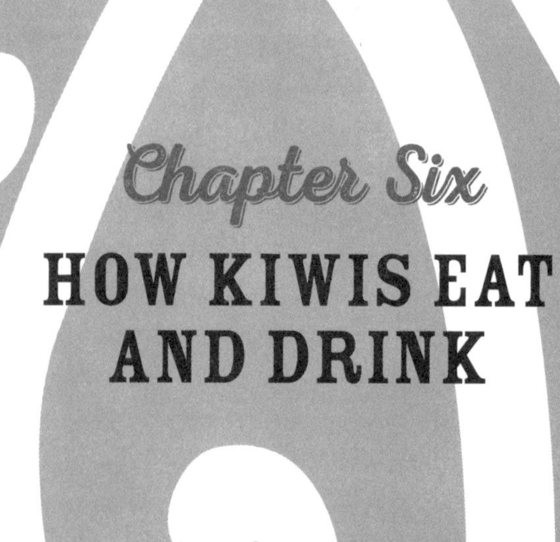

Chapter Six

HOW KIWIS EAT AND DRINK

Thank God for migrants. They rescued us from a diet too long favoured by descendants of English colonials: meat and three veg cooked to within an inch of its edible life.

In the 1960s, it led us to dabble with new concepts of sophistication. We wowed dinner guests with chicken-in-a-basket, rehydrated Surprise peas, and a salad drenched in condensed milk and vinegar. But under ongoing overseas influence (boosted by younger Kiwis returning from their OE), our national palate was steadily refreshed and retrained by novel flavours and styles of cooking.

In the '70s, we went a bit "continental" with wiener schnitzel, fondues and quiches. In the '80s, we experimented with the microwave, made our own muesli bars, and discovered that hummus and pesto could add pizzazz. The '90s brought nachos, balsamic drizzle, and kitchen inspiration from *Marvellous Muffins*.

By the turn of the century, our unshackled appetites were tackling eggplant and zucchini stacks, sushi, and paninis. A decade later, it was ramen noodles, pork banh mi, smashed avo, and turmeric lattes. Things that once would have baffled us had become mainstream.

Still, you can take the Kiwi out of New Zealand, but you can't entirely take . . .

Even Peter Gordon — the chef who made a global name with "fusion" cooking — admits he loves baking his mum's pavlova. It's the "kiwi thing" he most loves doing, he says. Yes, there has been a food revolution here. But there are some dishes we'll never give up. These are the icons of Kiwi home cooking.

- **Bacon-and-egg pie:** This is the Kiwi picnic classic. It can be as plain as bacon, eggs, and pastry; if you like, you can bulk out the basics with onion, cheese, spinach (or, heaven help us, peas). You'll find it at rugby sidelines, beach picnics, and casual lunches — the ultimate "she'll be right" food, filling and forgiving.

- **Lolly cake:** Edible nostalgia. A log of crushed malt biscuits, sweetened condensed milk, butter, and those garishly pink Eskimo lollies (now re-branded as "Explorers" after criticism of the name), rolled in coconut. Born in the 1950s and still a staple of suburban bakeries and school fairs.
- **Cheese rolls:** A reconstructed cheese sandwich, probably not a favourite with heart health specialists, but very popular for its comfort factor. A specialty of Southland and Otago. You slather a cheese filling over a slice of bread, then roll the bread up and toast it under the grill. Before the toast burns and just as the cheese becomes deliciously melted, it's done.
- **Whitebait fritters:** Whitebait are the tiny, translucent young of various freshwater fish — native to New Zealand, but still pricey. Best cooked in a small omelette and then eaten between two slices of white bread with a squeeze of lemon juice. The only impediment to enjoyment is that you have to ignore those little black eyes looking at you as you bite into the fritter. Enjoyed from September to November; not a year-round treat.
- **Pavlova:** A celebratory meringue-based dessert which must have a crispy crust and a slightly chewy centre. Traditionally topped with whipped cream and kiwifruit or summer berries. A Christmas tradition.
- **Sausage rolls:** Spiced-up sausage meat rolled in flaky pastry. Hearty, herby, and pleasingly greasy, sausage rolls are superior to any dainty hors d'oeuvre that crumbles

in your hand. Possibly the most popular offering of anybody asked to "bring a plate". Tomato sauce compulsory.

- **Cheese scones:** The best cheese scones are fluffy on the inside, crunchy on the outside, and especially good if a pinch of cayenne pepper has gone into the mix. Best eaten piping hot with butter melting into the crumb. The idea of including cheese in the mixture came from Scotland, but these scones are now as much a part of Kiwi café culture as the flat white.
- **ANZAC biscuits:** Oats, golden syrup and coconut, crisp at the edges and chewy in the middle. A recipe born of wartime practicality (the main ingredients wouldn't go stale during a long delivery to overseas soldiers), the name is legally protected. Commercial use is expected to honour the traditional name and recipe. Anzac biscuits are never, under any circumstances, to be called "cookies".

But Kiwis don't live entirely on bacon-and-egg pies and lolly cake. When it comes to eating out, our tastes have changed just as dramatically.

Dining out and taking away

Despite their loyalty to traditional treats, Kiwis were easily persuaded to start "going out for dinner". Many of those migrants who came here opened up restaurants and introduced us to their favourites from back home. In the 1970s, the height of exotic was chicken chow mein, sweet and sour pork, or fried rice, often served with white bread and butter on the side as Kiwi hedging against the unfamiliar. By the 1990s, butter chicken and naan were being devoured in suburban Indian restaurants, and not long after, Thai eateries popped up on high streets everywhere. The nation started talking about pad thai and green curry less like foreign imports and more like weeknight staples. Now, it's not hard to find Nepalese, Turkish and Filipino restaurants.

The global fast-food chains made an appearance, too. McDonald's, KFC and Pizza Hut landed in New Zealand from the 1970s onward, reshaping Friday nights and family meals.

A glass of wine with your dinner, madam?

Eating out was made even better when Otto Groen's dogged seven-year campaign petitioning lawmakers to change the liquor licensing rules finally succeeded. The breweries, hotels, churches and the Salvation Army had all been opposed, but eventually, on 13 December 1961, Groen's Auckland restaurant, The Gourmet, became the first in New Zealand to be granted a liquor licence under the Licensing Amendment Act 1961. Dining out was on the way to becoming a truly civilized experience.

Drinking through the decades

Ever since James Cook's sailors brewed up a rough-and-ready beer from rimu branches and mānuka leaves, booze has been part of the Kiwi lifestyle. In the pioneering days it caused no end of trouble, especially in Russell — then nicknamed the "Hellhole of the Pacific" for its grog shops, brawls and brothels.

That was until the wowsers arrived. The temperance movement gathered strength in the late 19th and early 20th centuries, determined to curb the country's drinking habits. They were influential enough to force through a law that shut the pub doors at six o'clock sharp each evening. Thus began the long, thirsty era of the infamous "six o'clock swill", when men crowded into pubs straight after work to get as much beer on board as possible before closing time.

Eventually, in 1967, and after 50 years, the government bowed to public pressure and abolished the archaic licensing law. It was a defining moment in the country's social history. From this point on, pubs could stay open until 10 p.m., and the way Kiwis drank and socialised changed for good.

By the 1970s and '80s, things began to loosen up further. Restaurants could finally serve alcohol. Marlborough sauvignon blanc was steadily replacing Müller-Thurgau as our preferred drop, and because it was permissible to order a glass of wine with your dinner, you no longer had to skulk home to your flagon or bottle of Cold Duck. At the same time, "chateau cardboard" — a cardboard box with a plastic bladder inside, complete with a handy tap — was becoming a pantry staple. It was the student flat's best friend. Thousands of Kiwis learned about "table wine" by squeezing the last dribbles out of a collapsing sack.

By the 1990s, we were going upmarket. The flat white had become the focal point of our coffee culture, cafés were dotted through every retail village, and New Zealand wine had gone from "cask convenience" to Central Otago pinot noir with an international price tag.

New Zealand was starting to show all the signs of having a problem with booze. We couldn't seem to grasp the continental style of moderation. Alcohol was implicated in a majority of road accidents; domestic violence was fuelled by it; heart disease and cancers could be attributed to it.

The statistics made us sit up and take notice. By the 2020s, something new was happening: young New Zealanders were drinking less than any generation before them. Dry July had gone mainstream, kombucha was on tap at cafés, and zero-percent beers were turning up at barbecues. Binge-drinking followed by chundering — once seen as a rite of passage — was starting to look more tragic than heroic.

Still, as journalist Steve Braunias wryly observed, "the plain fact of the matter is that for much of New Zealand, alcohol is good fun." And that's the paradox: we may drink less, or drink differently, but drinking still has a central place in the way Kiwis celebrate, commiserate and connect.

Icons of Kiwi drinking

1. Beer

Speight's if you're southern, Lion Red if you're northern, DB Draught if you like to argue about it. That's if you're a traditionalist. If you're not, there's a huge craft beer world to enjoy.

2. Wine

Marlborough sauvignon blanc ("sav blonk") put New Zealand wine on the world map. Central Otago pinot noir is our moody, expensive darling. Sam Neill makes a fine one under his Two Paddocks label. Its description is truly seductive: "Bramble, spice and wild herb aromatics sit gently on the nose, then lead to an elegant finely driven mouthfeel, showing poise, freshness and a lingering persistent finish."

3. Cask wine

The infamous cardboard box is still stocked on supermarket shelves. Equal parts social lubricant and social embarrassment, the cask was the backbone of many a 1980s party.

4. Soft drinks

Lemon & Paeroa — "World Famous in New Zealand". Still best with fish and chips on the beach, still proudly ours.

5. Hot drinks

Milo for the kids (or anyone after a winter's game of netball); a flat white for the grown-ups — our gift to global café culture, and still the best way to judge a Kiwi barista.

Socialising with Kiwis: Occasions for Sharing

Kiwis may try new tastes these days, but when it comes to socialising, a few food rituals remain non-negotiable. Here's the unspoken etiquette for our most iconic occasions:

The sausage sizzle

You'll find them outside hardware stores on a Saturday morning, at school fairs, sports clubs, even election day polling booths. For a gold coin, you get a slice of white bread, a sausage (sometimes still unnervingly pale), a squirt of tomato sauce, maybe a few fried onions if you're lucky. The etiquette? Don't sniff at the nation's nutritional preferences. It's called fundraising.

The backyard barbie

Every Kiwi home has a barbecue lurking somewhere, whether it's a rusty old flat-top or a gleaming stainless-steel beast. The rule of thumb is bring-your-own: your own meat, your own drinks. It's considered very bad form to turn up with half a dozen sausages and then eat someone else's butterflied lamb leg. Traditionally, it's men who do the cooking; women bring the salads and desserts. Make sure he's got a beer in his hand and accept that he might eventually cremate the sausages.

The boil-up

Born in Māori kitchens, the boil-up is hearty kai made from pork bones, potatoes, pūhā, watercress or cabbage, and doughboys (little dumplings). It's not fine dining, but it's filling, nourishing, and shared with whānau. If you're invited to join, the right response is simple: accept, eat up, and don't fuss. Compliment the cook — and remember, second helpings are a sign of respect.

The hāngī

The ultimate communal feast, cooked in an earth oven with hot stones. Meat, root vegetables and stuffing are wrapped and buried, then slowly steamed for hours. When the hāngī is lifted, everyone eats together. If you're a guest, don't expect restaurant plating — food will be served piled high and smoky. Etiquette? Join the line, take your share, and don't be shy about seconds.

The ultimate rule: *Bring a plate*

Whether it's a barbie, a birthday, or a work do, this phrase will appear again and again. Newcomers sometimes turn up clutching an empty plate, ready to be served. Wrong move. In Kiwi English, "bring a plate" means bring a plate *of food* to share — sausage rolls, cheese scones, whatever you can muster. Phone ahead of time to ask the host what would round out the menu they have in mind. It will avoid the awkwardness of only a bag of chips doing the rounds for a savoury course because everyone's turned up with a pavlova.

Saying grace

Sometimes, before the eating begins, Kiwis remember that food is more than fuel.

At many Māori gatherings, food is blessed with a simple karakia (prayer) before eating. One common version goes:

Whakapainga ēnei kai (*Bless these foods*)
Hei oranga mō te tinana (*For the well-being of our bodies*)
Mō ō mātou wairua (*And for our spirits*)
Āmine (*Amen*)

The Kiwi Burger

The year was 1991 and McDonald's had been operating in New Zealand for 15 years already, when Bryan Old, the owner of some McDonald's restaurants in Hamilton, wanted to add a new burger to the menu — one with a slice of beetroot and a fried egg besides the standard meat patty.

It took Bryan a long time to convince Head Office that this was a good idea.

Finally, on 22 October 1991, the new burger, called the "KiwiBurger", was advertised on TV for the first time. Unapologetically Kiwi, the ad presented the burger in a roll call of other icons of kiwiana . . . and it wasn't long before Kiwis would soon think of the KiwiBurger as an important icon of local culture.

New Zealand's drinking anthem

Th' Dudes' "Bliss" (1979) has become the great Kiwi drinking sing-along. It isn't poetry — just a chant about knocking back another round and forgetting the previous one. You don't so much sing it as bellow it, pint in hand, shoulder to shoulder with whoever's next to you. The song still breaks out at pubs, parties, and the odd rugby league game when the crowd decides it's time to let rip.

HERITAGE MOMENT

A name more befitting

15 June 1959: During the Cold War, New Zealand's "Chinese gooseberries" weren't exactly winning hearts in North America. The name carried too many political associations, and sales faltered. At a 1959 meeting of Turners and Growers, Auckland fruit auctioneer Jack Turner suggested a bold rebrand. Why not call the furry little fruit "kiwifruit"? Growers embraced it, and "kiwifruit" became the official name. Exports took off, turning the once-humble fruit into one of New Zealand's sweetest success stories. Today, kiwifruit is a billion-dollar industry and a staple in lunchboxes around the world.

Chapter Seven

HOW KIWIS PUSH PLAY

The national scorecard

What would we do on Saturdays without sport? Or any day, for that matter. Sport is stitched into the rhythm of our lives every day, every season, and every year. On warmer Saturday mornings, half the country seems to be strapping on cricket pads, fastening on a helmet, and keeping an eye on the wickets. On chillier mornings, half the country seems to be pulling on boots, slipping in mouthguards, pinning back hair, or packing chillybins for the sidelines. According to Sport New Zealand, around 92% of young people and 74% of adults take part in some form of sport or active recreation each week — which might explain why local parks are forever full of flying balls and determined little legs.

Sporting tastes shift with age and stage. At secondary schools, basketball, netball and rugby now jostle for the top spot, and basketball is catching up fast. Among adults, the choice widens: golf, tennis, cycling, running, surf lifesaving ... If it gets the heart rate up, someone here is doing it.

And when we're not playing, we're watching. All Blacks rugby tests still fill Eden Park to its 50,000-seat brim, the New Zealand Warriors now sell out their Go Media Stadium home games (averaging around 24,000 roaring fans), and football is muscling in on the big stage too. The Wellington Phoenix drew a record 33,000-strong crowd to their 2024 semifinal. Even if we can't all name the rules, we love the spectacle, the flags, the face paint, and the electric hum of a packed stadium.

Sailing has become a popular spectator sport, even among those who didn't grow up next to the water. The enthusiasm is contagious when Emirates Team New Zealand races for the America's Cup. The country watches and listens from waterfront fan zones or even just in front of their telly, and "foiling" becomes an essential vocabulary item. And while horse racing no longer dominates headlines as it once did, big meets like the New Zealand Trotting Cup still pull in the crowds, as much for the social whirl as the betting slip.

Our rugged backdrop also breeds niche passions: snowboarding, freestyle skiing and alpine skiing have all delivered Winter Olympic golds, while a loyal crew of petrol-heads keep motorsport roaring, from grassroots speedways to the global stage of Formula One. The name of Bruce McLaren lives on in one of the world's most famous racing teams.

In Aotearoa, sport isn't just recreation. It's where kids learn teamwork and discipline, a sports kit sparks loyalties, and national pride is cemented or shattered.

From grit to care: A new way of thinking

For decades, the defining image of New Zealand sport was toughness. Players were expected to carry on through pain, blood, and broken bones. Colin Meads famously played on with a fractured arm. Buck Shelford finished a test after having his scrotum torn (yes, really), and Richie McCaw led the All Blacks to World Cup victory while playing with a broken foot.

That was the culture: patch it up, get back out there, and prove you had enough mongrel in you to be a winner.

That attitude hasn't vanished, but it's no longer the standard. These days, a suspected concussion brings an instant sideline assessment. Players are stood down for head knocks, rested for overuse injuries, and monitored for mental fatigue. There's sports psychology support, nutritionists, and even mindfulness sessions — things that once would have been met with raised eyebrows and disparaging comments about "softness".

But not all new sporting trends are healthy. In 2025, some New Zealanders flew to Dubai to take part in Run It Straight, a conspicuously senseless head-on collision contest where two people sprint towards and smash into each other for prize money. After a 19-year-old in Palmerston North died following a backyard copy of the trend, concussion experts and trauma surgeons called for an immediate ban and warned of severe brain and spinal injury risk; even the Prime Minister weighed in.

Meanwhile, football's rise has gone the opposite way — built on inclusiveness rather than impact. Parents express relief that it has become a viable alternative to rugby at school level, boosted by the Football Ferns' history-making win over Norway at the 2023 FIFA Women's World Cup.

At the other end of the spectrum — and far kinder on the vertebrae — are the Manu World Championships, a celebratory take on the classic Kiwi "bomb", led largely by Māori and Pasifika communities. Competitors launch off wharves or diving platforms, land bottom-first, and chase the biggest, noisiest splash of the day. It's part skill, part theatre, and very New Zealand.

Some old-school fans miss the days of staunch sporting

brutes. Others are relieved to see brains and long-term well-being finally outranking bravado. Either way, the culture has shifted: "she'll be right" has given way to "are you all right?" — and that might be the biggest sign of civilised progress New Zealand sport has made.

Sporting colours

New Zealand's love affair with black began on a rugby field. In 1893, the newly formed New Zealand Rugby Football Union decided its national side would wear black jerseys with a silver fern, along with black socks and caps. It was a practical move — black dye was cheap and easy to match — but it also gave the team a unique identity.

When the All Blacks started storming through international rugby in the early 1900s, the black strip became famous, and the colour stuck fast to the national psyche. Over time, black and the silver fern became New Zealand's unofficial sporting livery, instantly recognisable anywhere in the world.

The haka

Some of the most familiar words in Māori belong to the haka Ka Mate, the challenge performed by the All Blacks before a rugby test. It has been part of their pre-match ritual for well over a century, first introduced to the rugby field by the pioneering "Originals" team who toured Britain in 1905-06 and won all but one of their matches.

For decades, though, the haka was treated more as a formality than a fierce cultural expression — until Buck Shelford became captain in 1987. He insisted the team perform it properly: with precision, power, and intent. Since then, the haka has become a mesmerising spectacle. It unsettles opponents, stirs up patriotic fervour in the stands, and primes the players for the clash to come.

Ā, ka mate! Ka mate! — 'Tis death! 'Tis death!
Ka ora! Ka ora! — 'Tis life! 'Tis life!
Tēnei te tangata pūhuruhuru — Behold the hairy man
Nāna nei i tiki mai whakawhiti te rā — who caused the sun to shine!

"Ka Mate" was composed about 200 years ago by Te Rauparaha, a fighting chief of Ngāti Toa. It celebrates his escape from enemies by hiding in a pit used for storing kūmara (sweet potato).

By the early 2000s, the time felt right for a haka that spoke more directly to what the players were about to do on the field. Enter Derek Lardelli of Ngāti Porou, a renowned tā moko (traditional tattoo) artist and cultural advisor. In 2005 he composed "Kapa o Pango", a new haka created specifically for the All Blacks. When the team first performed it against the Springboks at Carisbrook in Dunedin, some spectators were stunned — especially when Piri Weepu finished with what looked like a throat-slitting gesture. Lardelli quickly explained: the final gesture symbolised drawing energy across the body through the heart and lungs, not violence.

Kapa o Pango kia whakawhenua au i ahau! — Let me become one with the land
Hi aue, hī! Ko Aotearoa e ngunguru nei! — It is New Zealand that thunders now
Au, au, aue hā! — It is my time! It is my moment!

Ko Kapa o Pango e ngunguru nei! — This defines us as the All Blacks

Women and Māori/Pasifika in Sport

Women's sport has surged from a minority interest to centre stage. The Black Ferns lit up New Zealand with their triumphant Rugby World Cup campaign in 2017, defending their title in front of roaring home crowds. The White Ferns took out the 2000 Women's Cricket World Cup and lifted the ICC Women's T20 World Cup in 2024, while the Football Ferns claimed victory in the first match of the FIFA Women's World Cup finals in 2023. Coverage of women's sport, once barely visible, has jumped from about 15% to 27% of mainstream sports media.

Māori and Pasifika athletes form the backbone of many national teams, from the All Blacks and Black Ferns to netball, league, sevens and more. Their influence reaches well beyond athletic ability. They bring waiata and haka to opening ceremonies, reo and slang to team cultures, and a sense of whanaungatanga — kinship and collective strength — to the way New Zealand plays.

Boardrooms and commentary boxes haven't caught up yet. Women and Māori/Pasifika voices are still under-represented in sports governance and media, but their impact on the field is impossible to miss.

Names to drop

Every sport has its legends — names Kiwis instinctively reach for when the subject comes up. If you can nod knowingly when these names surface, you'll sound like you've got your priorities straight (and earned full Kiwi credentials).

If You're Going to Talk About . . .	You've Got to Mention . . .	Because . . .
Rugby	Richie McCaw	Captained the All Blacks to back-to-back Rugby World Cup wins (2011, 2015)
Netball	Dame Noeline Taurua	Celebrated coach of the Silver Ferns controversially sidelined in 2025
Cricket	Kane Williamson	Led the Black Caps to the 2021 ICC World Test Championship title
Football	Hannah Wilkinson	Scored the Football Ferns' first-ever World Cup goal (2023)
Basketball	Steven Adams	NBA star; proof New Zealand can produce NBA giants
Para-swimming	Dame Sophie Pascoe	New Zealand's most successful Paralympian
Rugby league	Roger Tuivasa-Sheck	Plays as a winger or fullback for the NZ Warriors
Athletics	Hamish Kerr	Olympic and world champion high-jump medallist
Canoeing	Dame Lisa Carrington	New Zealand's most decorated Olympian (eight golds, one bronze)
Golf	Dame Lydia Ko	Won her first LPGA event at 15; former world No. 1
Softball	Mark Sorenson	Led the Black Sox to multiple world titles

Tennis	Michael Venus	French Open doubles champion, Olympic bronze medalist
Lawn bowls	Jo Edwards	Double Commonwealth Games gold
Sailing	Sir Peter Blake	Skippered Team NZ to America's Cup glory (1995); murdered in the Amazon in 2001
Snowboarding	Zoi Sadowski-Synnott	NZ's first Winter Olympic gold (2022)
Boxing	Joseph Parker	Holder of the World Boxing Organization interim heavyweight title since 2024
Alpine skiing	Alice Robinson	Youngest-ever FIS World Cup GS winner
Freestyle skiing	Nico Porteous	Won Olympic gold in the halfpipe (2022); our youngest ever Winter Olympic medalist
Running	Sam Ruthe	The world's youngest person to run a sub-four-minute mile
Shot put	Tom Walsh	The seventh best shot putter in history
Formula One	Liam Lawson	Impressed on debut; variable performance since then

Local knowledge: A sporting colour code

All Blacks: men's rugby union
Beach Blacks: men's beach volleyball
Black Dragons: dragon boat
Black Ferns: women's rugby union
Black Foils: SailGP team
Black Jacks: men's and women's lawn bowls
Black Caps: men's cricket
Black Sox: men's softball
Black Sticks: men's and women's field hockey
Ice Blacks: men's ice hockey
E Blacks: Esports
Volley Blacks: men's volleyball
Tall Blacks: men's basketball
Wheel Blacks: wheelchair rugby
Black Fins: surf lifesaving
Iron Blacks: American football or gridiron

- Curious point no. 1: The national soccer team is called the All Whites.
- Curious point no. 2: For a few months, the men's badminton team called itself the Black Cocks, until the International Badminton Federation put its foot down and the name was officially dropped.

A Whistle for the Ref

In Wellington on 26 June 1884, referee William Atack made sporting history. While officiating a rugby match between senior sides from Canterbury and Wellington, he became the first known referee in the world to use a whistle to control a game. Until then, referees had to shout to stop play — often ignored over the roar of the crowd and the clash of players. Atack's quick blast on a brass whistle cut clean through the noise. The idea caught on fast, spreading through New Zealand and the wider rugby world — and today, no sport on earth starts without it.

HERITAGE MOMENT

Arthur Porritt runs with Harold Abrahams at the Paris Olympics

At the Paris Olympics in 1924, Arthur Porritt races against Harold Abrahams in the 100-metre sprint. The English runner wins the gold; the Kiwi wins bronze. This is the race that will be immortalised in the film *Chariots of Fire*, but out of modesty, Porritt does not allow his name to be mentioned in the movie. His character is instead called Tom Watson. Abrahams and Porritt forged a lifelong friendship. Every year thereafter, on 7 July at 7:00 pm — the exact time and date of the race — the Porritts and the Abrahams met for dinner. Porritt went on to become New Zealand's first Kiwi-born Governor-General in 1967.

Chapter Eight

THE KIWI LANGUAGE

If you thought you knew English, your first few days in New Zealand might have made you doubt your hearing. Kiwis speak fast and are prone to mumble. We say *eh* and *y'know* all the time, and in a regrettable (but thankfully rare) moment of grammar lapse, we might address you as "youse", even when there's nobody else around.

Vowel issues...

Our accent is cause for mirth, according to outsiders. People say we call our country *New Zillund*, or *In Zid* (for short). When we agree with something, we say *yiss*. Australians tell us that when we want to buy six fish, we ask for *sucks fush*. (They're exaggerating. Typical Aussies ...) But it's true that we grow our own *vidgies* in the back garden and keep our tools in the *shid*. And a double "ll" at the end of a word can disappear completely. If we hear you're under the weather, we'll hope you "Git wee-uh soon".

One visitor who walked the Te Araroa Trail — a 3,000km hike stretching the length of Aotearoa — noted on Facebook that a fellow Kiwi tramper had informed him he'd have "strong leeks" by the end of the walk.

But our vowels can cause real confusion. Koos Turenhout, a South African migrant, recalled arriving in New Zealand to find his house had a power issue. A neighbour told him, "Yeah, nah. Call Victor. Victor needs to sort that out." Later, a parent at school gave the same advice about a power pole blocking the family's view. Turenhout began to wonder who this influential "Victor" might be. Only later did he discover that "Victor" was in fact Vector, the local power company.

Are you listening?

What baffles many new listeners to New Zealand is that we often let our sentences go up at the end, even when we're not asking a question. This feature isn't unique to New Zealand; you'll also hear it in parts of Australia, California, Canada, and even Ireland. In those places, too, speakers let their pitch rise at the end of a statement. But we're not asking you anything. It's our way of saying, "Are you following? Does that make sense?" If you ask us to explain the haka, for example, we might say: "I guess the whole point of the haka is to *unsettle the opposition*? It makes the players look *aggressive*?" On the page it looks hesitant, but what we're really doing is checking you're still with us.

Outrageously charming

It turns out we don't just sound funny to outsiders; we sound *irresistible*. In 2019, the travel site Big 7 Travel polled 8,500 people from 60 countries, and the New Zealand accent came in at number 1 out of 50. Yes, officially the *sexiest accent in the world*. We'll take it.

Te Reo Māori — it's official

Along with our warped vowels, our idiosyncratic intonation, and our baffling lexicon, there's another feature of Kiwi language that sometimes takes newcomers unaware. It's the frequency with which you'll hear Māori inserted unapologetically into everyday conversation. Meetings will start with a Māori greeting; government departments have Māori names; evening news broadcasts begin their announcement in Māori . . . You'll see and hear words like *mahi* and *mana*, *whānau* and *whakapapa*, across all kinds of public settings — from school assemblies and council documents to job descriptions and staff meetings.

You won't always find a translation. Some words are so embedded in the national conversation that it's assumed everyone understands their meaning.

Here's a starter pack of 30 words in te reo Māori

1. hui	meeting
2. iti	little
3. ka pai!	very good; well done!
4. kai	food
5. karakia	prayer
6. kaupapa	a principle or policy
7. Kia ora !	Hi! G'day! Also thank you.
8. Kirihimete	Christmas
9. kōrero	discussion
10. mahi	work, job
11. mana	authority, influence, spiritual power, charisma
12. manuhiri	guests, visitors
13. Māoritanga	things that relate directly to Māori values and concepts
14. marae	traditional meeting place
15. moko	traditional tattoo on the face or body
16. mokopuna	grandchild or young person
17. nui	big
18. Pākehā	people of European origin; non-Māori

19. pounamu	greenstone
20. rangatahi	young people
21. tamariki	children
22. tāne	man, husband
23. tangihanga	funeral
24. taniwha	guardian; legendary monster
25. taonga	treasured possessions or cultural items
26. tikanga Māori	the Māori way of doing things, practices, conventions
27. tūrangawaewae	the place where you have the right to live because of whakapapa
28. wahine	woman; wife
29. waiata	song or chant
30. waka	boat or canoe; car or airplane; sometimes used figuratively to mean a political party

The resurgence of te reo Māori (the Māori language) in everyday life has been powerful. For decades, the language was actively suppressed. Māori children were punished for speaking it at school, and many grew up without learning the language of their ancestors. But attitudes have done a one-eighty. Māori was declared an official language of New Zealand on 1 August 1987, and at the same time, the Māori Language Commission (Te Taura Whiri i te Reo Māori) was established to actively promote the language.

And it's working. According to the 2023 General Social Survey (which looks at those aged 15 and above), more than one in five New Zealanders (22%) are learning or have tried to learn te reo Māori, and nearly 9% of the population say they can have a conversation in it. When you're job-hunting, fluency may not be a necessity, but it's definitely an asset.

Depends how you read it

Of course, there are the nay-sayers. You might hear a few unpleasant gripes about "Maorification" — this increased influence of the Māori language — but those who complain about "excessive" and "inappropriate" inclusion of Māori language in public life are hastily muted.

In August 2025, the media reported that the Minister for Education, Erica Stanford, had instructed officials to reduce or remove the use of Māori words from books used in primary schools to help five-year-olds learn to read. The move sparked widespread criticism, with many seeing it as a step backwards in normalising te reo in everyday life.

What did you just say?

Separated so long from the mothership, our speaking has naturally evolved in response to local conditions, and we've ended up with a vocabulary enriched with a few linguistic oddities.

Here's a decoder for a few items of the local jargon. A note of caution, though: some slang disappears faster than a jandal floating on a riptide, and you risk looking silly — a "try hard" — if you misjudge their meaning or the context.

That said, there are a few hardy perennials that should (eventually) form part of your working vocabulary:

- Have a good one! — I hope your day goes well.
- She'll be right — everything's going to be fine.
- Yeah, nah — I hear what you're saying, but I'm not sure if I agree with you.
- All good — don't worry, everything's okay.

- Choice! — excellent, great.
- Bro — mate, dude (not just for brothers).
- Tu meke! — too much (used to show praise or amazement).
- Heaps — lots.
- Mean! — awesome, excellent.
- Booze bus — a roadside checkpoint where police stop drivers to check if they have been drinking alcohol.
- Budgie smugglers — men's skimpy, tight swimwear (think about it).
- Couch kumara — a person who sits on the couch watching television for hour after hour, no more animated than the vegetable itself.
- Fair go — a situation where reasonable expectations are met — on both sides; for example, "It's not a fair go expecting me to clear up all your mess."
- Flash — flash clothes or a flash restaurant might be regarded with suspicion as being excessively sophisticated or fashionable. On the other hand, if you "don't feel too flash", you don't feel very well.
- Mental health day: a day off work, taken not because you're physically sick but because you feel that time spent relaxing would be beneficial to your attitude; don't expect your employer to sympathise or approve.
- OE — overseas experience — an extended working holiday abroad, usually for a year or two after graduating from university, and often starting in London, England. Also referred to as "the big OE".
- Op shop — opportunity shop; thrift store; a shop where second-hand clothes and other goods are sold to raise money for charity.
- Pack a sad — to slump into sadness or despair. If a Kiwi

packs a sad, it might well be because the All Blacks have just lost. If a machine packs a sad, it has stopped working.

- Sausage sizzle — a fundraising barbecue where sausages are cooked on the barbie, wrapped in white bread and sold (with the option of fried onions and tomato sauce) for a dollar or two.
- She'll be right — everything will be okay; sometimes abbreviated to "She's right."
- Shout — if it's your shout at the pub, then it's your turn to buy a round of drinks for everybody. If somebody shouts you to the movies, they are paying for your ticket.
- The Big One — a term to describe a severe earthquake that citizens of Wellington fear will inevitably occur one day.
- Togs — swimwear.
- To be up at sparrow fart — to get out of bed very early in the morning.
- Waka jumper — a politician who switches his support from one party (*waka* = canoe) to another.
- Wasted — severely affected by alcohol or drugs.
- Yeah, right — a sarcastic snort of disbelief. The phrase became popular following a series of topical billboard advertisements for Tui beer; for example: "Let's take a

moment this Christmas to think about Christ." "Yeah, right."

Use these sparingly until you've sussed the situation. Listening is a better first move.

Reading between the lines

Kiwis have mastered the art of understatement. Gushing over-enthusiasm (when things are good) sounds crass to our ears, and maudlin over-dramatisation (when things are bad) is called "packing a sad".

Remember when Sir Edmund Hillary came down from Mt Everest, the first man to climb the world's highest mountain? He turned to a mate and simply said, "Well, George, we knocked the bastard off." Since that feat in 1953, he's remained the person Kiwis trust most.

We get around expressing excess emotion by saying the opposite of what we mean. Well, we *do* say what we mean, but you might have to turn it upside down to understand it. You might hear someone say, "Too easy!" just before they tackle something horrendous. You're meant to proffer a wry smile and admire the lack of melodrama; you don't have to spout sympathy in response. To see how this works in practice, study the translation in each case below:

- "It wasn't too shabby." → It was actually excellent.
- "They're not in any hurry with the drinks, are they?" → The service is ridiculously slow.
- "He's no idiot." → He's smart and competent.
- "It's not the worst flat I've lived in." → It's actually one of the better ones.

- "That's not a bad idea." → You're a genius.
- "I've had worse meals." → This was tasty.
- "Well, she's no spring chicken." → Crikey, she's old!
- "Not bad, eh?" → It's pretty good, right?
- "Bit of a character, that one." → Watch out, he's a real handful.

Once you learn to read between the lines, you'll realise Kiwis often say the opposite of what they mean. Listen closely and remain nimble.

Can you see the joke?

Kiwi humour is a specialist field of applied linguistics. It's quirky and always described as self-deprecating.

Before streaming, TikTok, and global stand-up specials, we had some much-adored comedy caricatures who made us laugh with their no-holds-barred observations of Kiwi life — our race relations, the urban-rural divide, and the differences between male and female. In our splendid back-blocks isolation, we found ourselves very funny.

The jokes don't always leap off the page, but it's well worth Googling these names to find video clips of their shows.

Fred Dagg (a.k.a. John Clarke)

Wearing a singlet, stubbies, gumboots and a floppy hat — and always speaking in a laconic drawl — Fred Dagg was the archetypal Kiwi farmer. He was helped on his farm by his seven sons, all named Trevor. Clarke's priceless satire savagely critiqued the absurdity of some of our local politicians.

Billy T James

Billy T wore a black singlet and shorts and a bright yellow towel around his neck to read the news. We held our breath as he poked fun at our somewhat disastrous race relations. Should we really make a joke of that, we wondered? Is he making us laugh at Māori people? We adored him for it. You'll hear echoes of that kind of humour in Taika Waititi's film *Boy* (2010), where characters speak in a recognisable Māori English accent.

McPhail and Gadsby

David McPhail and Jon Gadsby were the sharpest satirists of their time, skewering politicians and puffed-up personalities on *A Week of It* (1977–79) and *McPhail & Gadsby*. McPhail later said that showing Muldoon on television in caricature proved that the nation had become "mature" — capable of facing its anxieties and fears not by silence, but by satire.

Footrot Flats (by Murray Ball)

Not a person but a comic strip — and later a beloved animated film — *Footrot Flats* told the story of Wal, a gruff Kiwi bloke, and his loyal (but opinionated) sheepdog, known only as Dog. Their muddy farm life was full of mishaps, stubborn animals, and stifled feelings.

They're gone, but when the old clips resurface, we laugh as if nothing's changed.

We have to assume this is an Australian joke

(Warning: If you're of a prudish disposition, look away now.)
"I asked a Kiwi how many sexual partners he had had . . . He fell asleep counting."

HERITAGE MOMENT

Why don't you say how you really feel?

17 March 1999: When Emirates Team New Zealand lost the 2013 America's Cup yacht race in San Francisco Bay after coming so tantalisingly close to winning, Prime Minister John Key tweeted a single word: "Bugger". We're allowed to say this rude word, because the Advertising Standards Authority (ASA) says so. Back in 1999, the ASA had to consider a complaint about an advertisement on TV in which a series of farming mishaps, caused by underestimating the power of a Toyota Hi-Lux ute, prompted the farmer and his wife to express their vexation in the same single potent word: "Bugger!" Even the farm dog said it when he was left sprawling in the mud after missing his leap onto the back of the truck. The ad raised eyebrows in more than a few suburban living rooms, but the ASA dismissed complaints by saying "the usage of a Kiwi colloquialism is appropriate to the circumstances portrayed". Losing the America's Cup by one miserable point created similarly appropriate circumstances.

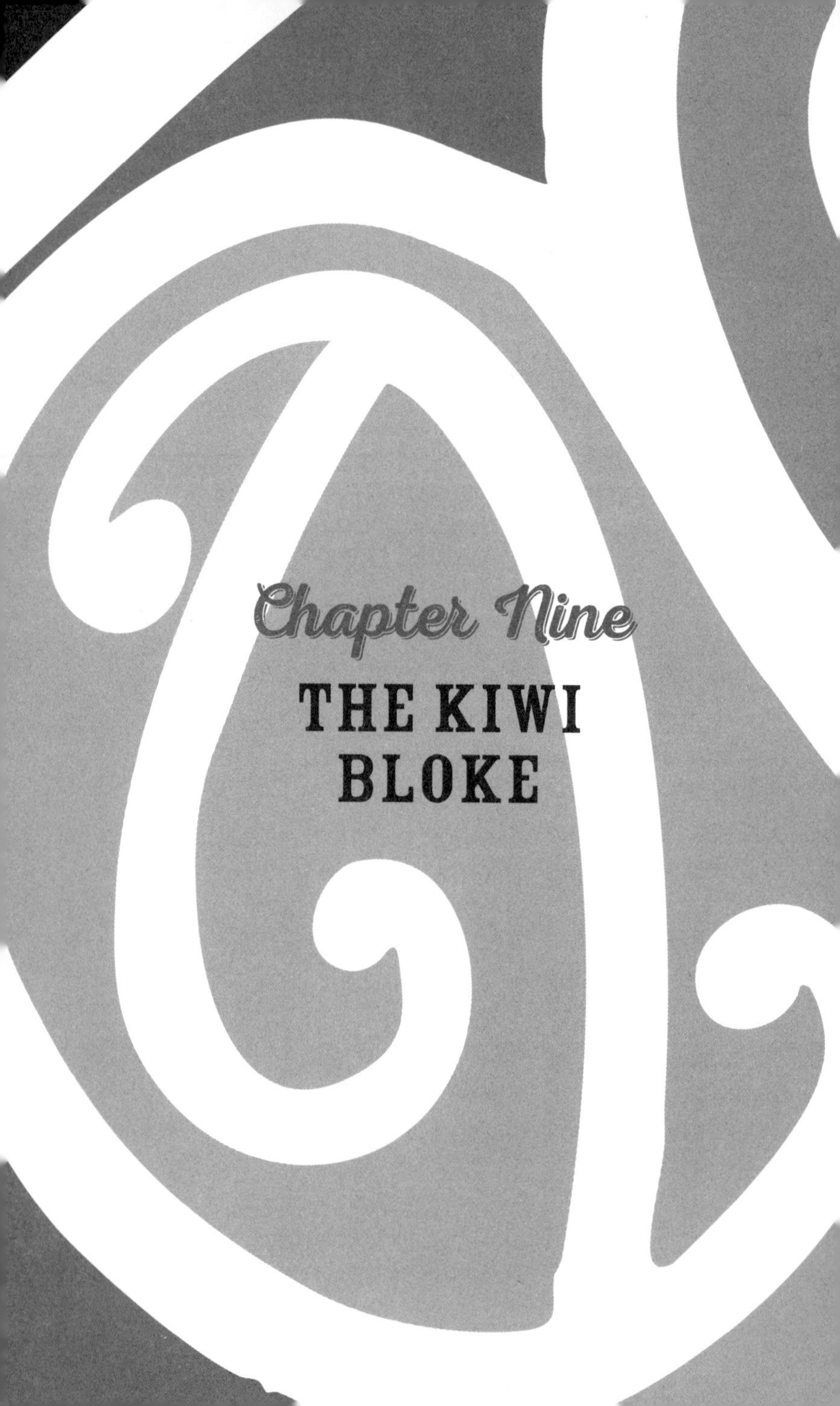

Chapter Nine

THE KIWI BLOKE

The Kiwi bloke has long laboured under an inhibiting stereotype.

Supposedly, he's the guy in stubbies and steelcapped boots, beer in one hand and barbecue tongs in the other. He probably played rugby once, or says he would have if not for the knee. His speech tone is flat. He gets jumpy around gushy emotions and needs a nudge to look after his health. He has mates, but the intimacy of their chat is underwhelming. He finds time in his shed more therapeutic than any session with a psychologist.

Behind that image sits an older archetype: the "man alone", a solitary settler or bushman, self-sufficient and stoic, with only the land and a dog for company. Especially after World War I, our heroes were those who knew when to "man up" and mask pain or fear. The good Kiwi bloke became silent, independent, emotionally unavailable.

That caricature still roams the provinces, although sightings are becoming increasingly rare. You might spot him at the A&P Show or leaning on a race at a shearing shed, but the reality today is more complicated. The Kiwi male is a varied species. Alongside a predictable career choice, he might also coach netball, wear merino thermals, do the school run and make a mean Thai green curry. He might grow dahlias, cry at *Tinā*, or volunteer for the mental health charity that once helped him. In fact, the real Kiwi bloke is often emotionally astute, deeply loyal, and quietly progressive — just not always eager to advertise it.

"He's a good bloke," people say admiringly, and it means he's solid. Reliable. He probably *does* "I love you" rather than *says* it. He helps you move house without complaining. He turns up with jumper cables when your battery dies. He doesn't seek praise and probably doesn't say too much, full stop. But silence isn't simplicity. Embrace a Kiwi bloke and you'll find loyalty, courage, sacrifice, generosity, devotion, endurance — even vulnerability.

Vigilance: Rob Hall

Rob Hall, one of our leading mountaineers, guided dozens of clients to Himalayan summits. In May 1996, a violent storm struck Everest. Near the South Summit, client Doug Hansen was too weak to descend. Hall stayed. Frostbitten and out of options, he radioed Base Camp and spoke to his pregnant wife, Jan Arnold, on the satphone. Summoning his last strength, he told her, "Sleep well, my sweetheart. Please don't worry too much." He died still tethered to the client he refused to abandon.

Sacrifice: Grant Kereama

By the early 2000s, Jonah Lomu's rare kidney disease left him gravely ill. In 2004, close friend and radio broadcaster Grant Kereama offered a kidney: "I had two kidneys and was in great health. Jonah was not well and needed one. It was simple for me." The transplant bought Lomu precious years with his whānau and fans. Kereama slipped back to work, never seeking the spotlight.

Fearlessness: Willie Apiata

On 17 June 2004 in Afghanistan, New Zealand SAS soldiers came under a predawn attack. One trooper suffered life-threatening arterial bleeding. Willie Apiata hoisted him and carried him, as his citation would read, "across seventy metres of broken, rocky and fireswept ground", fully exposed to enemy fire, to safety. He rearmed and returned to the fight. He became the first — and so far only — recipient of the Victoria Cross for New Zealand, insisting he'd simply done what a man does for his mates. (Charlie Upham, VC and Bar, received the Victoria Cross, since renamed.)

Mateship: Senior Constable Dave Robison and Police Dog Ice

For nearly two decades, Senior Constable Dave Robison worked with his patrol dog, Ice - fierce tracker on duty, gentle crowd pleaser off it. In Kawerau, the pair cornered a violent offender; Ice stayed on task and brought him down. Off the clock, he visited schools and soaked up hugs. In 2016, Ice won both the National Patrol Dog Championship and the Australasian title. When he died in retirement in 2021, Robison called him "a mate out of the box".

Tribute: Rob Hamill

In 2009, rower Rob Hamill stood in a Phnom Penh courtroom to confront the Khmer Rouge commander responsible for his brother Kerry's death. Kerry had been captured in 1978 when his yacht strayed into Cambodian waters, tortured at Tuol Sleng, then murdered. For three decades the family carried the grief. In court, Rob described Kerry as his "gorgeous, beautiful brother" and spoke for an hour about the devastation the killing had caused. He urged the world to "take notice of the evil that can happen when people do nothing". His testimony became part of the tribunal's record that convicted Duch of crimes against humanity.

Advocacy: Mike King

For years, comedian Mike King played the clown while battling depression and addiction. In the mid 2000s, he dropped the mask and became one of our most visible mental health advocates. He founded the Key to Life Charitable Trust and launched I Am Hope and Gumboot Friday, opening up free counselling for youth. Blunt and funny, he helped young men talk about struggles they'd long kept silent. King attracted storms. He resigned from the Ministry of Health's suicide advisory panel in 2017, calling its strategy "a masterclass in butt covering". In 2024, he was criticised for suggesting alcohol sometimes prevented suicides. For all the friction, he changed the national conversation: vulnerability isn't weakness; speaking out saves lives.

Devotion: Hudson and Halls

Peter Hudson and David Halls became household names with their camp, chaotic cooking show *Hudson and Halls* (1976–86). Offscreen they were life partners, though in those days nobody said so out loud. "Are we gay? Well, we're certainly merry," they quipped. In 1990 they moved to London. In September 1992, Hudson died of prostate cancer with Halls at his side. Fourteen months later Halls died by suicide, a photo of Peter in his hand and this note in his diary: "Without Peter I don't want to go on — he was my life . . . I want to be with him for all eternity."

Endurance: Bob Blair

On 24 December 1953, the Tangiwai rail disaster killed 151 people when a lahar destroyed a bridge and the Overnight Express train plunged into the Whangaehu River. Among the muddy bodies dragged from the river was Nerissa Love, fiancée of cricketer Bob Blair. In Johannesburg the next day, the New Zealand team faced South Africa in a test match. Blair, just 21, who had been told of her death, remained at the hotel, too distraught to join his team. The game was full of injury — Bert Sutcliffe was forced to play with a bandaged head — and the ninth wicket fell with the score at only 154. Suddenly the crowd rose, standing in silent ovation, as a solitary figure emerged from the tunnel. Sutcliffe put his arm around Blair's shoulders before the pair smashed 25 runs off a single over.

Defender: Sir Robert "Bom" Gillies

Sir Robert "Bom" Gillies, last surviving member of the 28th (Māori) Battalion, enlisted underage and fought in Italy. Wounded, he returned to serve, embodying the battalion motto, "Ake ake kia kaha e!" ("Forever and ever be strong.") After the war he quietly championed Māori veterans' welfare. Long reluctant to accept honours, he took a knighthood in 2022, saying, "There are many soldiers who did more and have never been recognised. I accept on behalf of all the boys." He died aged 99 on 7 November 2024.

The Agony of Love: Nigel "No Mates"

A gannet dubbed "the loneliest bird in the world" lived on Mana Island off the coast at Porirua, amid a colony of nearly 80 replica birds that conservationists had installed to encourage other gannets to join him. Nigel loved — *really* loved — his concrete friends, and for four years, he tried valiantly to woo one of them by constructing a nest of seaweed, mud and twigs. His love was never requited. News of his sudden death at the end of January 2018, just as three real birds had joined the colony, reverberated around the world and even inspired a poem. Nigel was found dead in the nest that he had made for his "partner".

Blokes We're Not So Sure About

As in any whānau, some individuals we embrace and some we'd prefer stayed out of sight. Some tell embarrassing jokes. But they're still part of our whakapapa. These blokes sit in a murky corner of the imagination — acquitted yet doubted, convicted yet protesting innocence, suspected for no good reason, or maybe possessed of a questionable sense of humour. Each one here has their supporters, but also plenty of detractors.

Barry Crump

For years the face of the Hilux ads with Scotty, Barry Crump perfected the laconic bushman yarn and turned the backblocks voice into a mainstream identity. From adventures in the outdoors he amassed a treasury of hunting and fishing tales to tell, which he published in books with titles such as *A Good Keen Man* and *Bastards I Have Met*. Along the way, he married five times and fathered nine sons. Two years after his death, the documentary *A Wandering Star* (1999) shed uncompromising light on Crumpy's despicable abuse of women. The accounts from former partners still sit uneasily alongside his enduring popularity and sales success.

David Bain

Convicted in 1995 for the murder of his mother, his father, his two sisters and his younger brother, David Bain protested his innocence, saying he was out on his paper run when the killings took place. His supporters believed David's father, Robin, was responsible. David's convictions were quashed by the Privy Council in 2007; he was acquitted at a retrial in 2009. A long fight over compensation followed: one retired judge said he was innocent on the balance of probabilities; another reviewer disputed the reasoning; the government declined compensation but made an ex gratia payment for costs. The public still wonders: wrongfully accused son or guilty man set free?

Paul Henry

A broadcaster known for on air provocations. In October 2010, during a TVNZ *Breakfast* interview with Prime Minister John Key, he questioned whether Governor General Sir Anand Satyanand was "even a New Zealander". In the days that followed, attention returned to a separate clip already in circulation in which Henry ridiculed the name of Delhi Chief Minister Sheila Dikshit during Commonwealth

Games coverage; India lodged a diplomatic protest. Henry apologised and resigned from TVNZ on 10 October. Supporters said he was a victim of political correctness; others said only the lowest common denominator would find him funny. In June 2025, TVNZ chose Henry to host a four-episode series, *The Chase New Zealand*.

Kim Dotcom

German-born internet entrepreneur whose life in Aotearoa has been part court case, part public theatre. After the armed 2012 raid on his Coatesville mansion at the request of the FBI, he became the face of a sprawling extradition battle over his Megaupload empire. Supporters cast him as a free speech innovator standing up to US overreach and to New Zealand's own missteps (the unlawful GCSB surveillance and apology). Critics see a showman who built a fortune on other people's work and then gamed the system. He launched the Internet Party in 2014, released music, hosted fireworks — and kept fighting. A symbol, depending on your seat, of audacity or excess.

Scott Watson

Watson was convicted of the New Year's Day 1998 murders of Ben Smart and Olivia Hope in the Marlborough Sounds. Their bodies were never found. Watson maintained his innocence, while debate raged over the reliability of the memory of a water taxi driver who was the last to see the young friends, and the handling of forensic fragments such as blonde hair linked by DNA testing to Olivia. Appeals, reviews and arguments have kept the case in the headlines;

in September 2025, the Court of Appeal declined to quash his convictions. His father described the outcome as "pretty much business as usual for him."

Philip Polkinghorne

In 2024, Auckland eye surgeon Philip Polkinghorne stood trial for the murder of his wife, Pauline Hanna, who had died three years earlier in their Remuera home. The defence argued it was a tragic suicide; in disbelief, friends and family insisted Pauline would never have done that. As the prosecution probed Polkinghorne's private life — rampant methamphetamine use and frequent visits to sex workers — the country watched, agog, and former patients were left mouthing "Gosh . . .". The jury returned a verdict of "not guilty". Legal innocence stands; public debate mutters on.

Brian Tamaki

Leader of Destiny Church. Instantly recognisable: an all black wardrobe, slicked back hair, dark shades, and a large motorbike. He came to national prominence with the 2004 Enough is Enough march against civil unions. In November 2016, days after the Kaikōura quake, he preached that earthquakes were divine punishment for national sins, naming homosexuals and murderers. In June 2025, at a Queen Street rally, his followers tore up flags of other faiths. Supporters say Destiny and its Man Up programme give some Māori men and youth a path away from gangs and drugs; critics see a polarising campaigner who extorts his followers for money to fund a lavish lifestyle.

Well-being

- Longevity: A boy born in 2020–22 can expect to live 80.5 years (girls 84.0).
- By ethnicity: Life expectancy at birth — Māori men about 73.4; Pacific men about 75.4.
- Suicide burden: Roughly 2.5 times as many men die by suicide as women.

Employment

- On the tools: Construction remains heavily male — about 84% of workers.
- In caring roles: Only 8%–9% of nurses are male; fewer than 5% of early-childhood teachers.
- Solo dads: About 24,600 of about 138,000 sole parent families with dependent children are father led (17.8%).
- Time off for family: Fewer than 1% of fathers take paid parental leave; only about 4% take unpaid leave. Stay at home dads remain rare.

Lifestyle/Civic life

- Showing up: In a 2023 survey, 47.5% of men had volunteered in the past four weeks.
- Behind bars: As of 30 June 2025, 9,966 men were in prison (92.4% of the prison population).
- Changing behaviour: In 2024, courts recorded 2,592 completions of nonviolence programmes by people whose offending included violence.

The Dad Who Broods

In two kiwi species — the little spotted kiwi and the North Island brown kiwi — the male incubates the egg. After the female lays an enormous egg — up to a fifth of her body weight — she leaves to recover. The male sits for 75–90 days, seldom leaving the burrow, losing weight as he warms and protects the chick. The kiwi dad's long vigil has become a symbol of the lengths to which a Kiwi dad will go to look after their family.

HERITAGE MOMENT

Conquering Everest

At 11:30 a.m. on 29 May 1953, Edmund Hillary of New Zealand and Tenzing Norgay of Nepal became the first men to reach the summit of Mount Everest. Their achievement made headlines around the world and brought pride to a small nation far away. Sir Ed devoted the rest of his life to helping the Sherpa people of Nepal, using his international celebrity to raise fund to build many schools and hospitals. He did much more than give Kiwis something to be proud of, though. His example — of humility, no matter how magnificent the achievement — became ingrained in the national psyche as the hallmark of a decent Kiwi. Sir Ed never revealed whether he or Tenzing was the first up there; only years later did Tenzing reveal it was Hillary. As Sam Neill described Sir Ed: "Quiet, decent, and yet extraordinary."

Chapter Ten

THE KIWI SHEILA

The "Kiwi bloke" has long been a fixture in our imagination — beer in hand, rugby on the screen, lawnmower waiting in the shed. But the Kiwi sheila? If we're looking for a stereotype, we've got a hard job on our hands.

Let's start with the obvious: Why "sheila"? That's an Aussie descriptor. The fact is, we had to borrow it because there isn't a true Kiwi female counterpart for "bloke". And that's her strength. She hasn't stopped in one position long enough to be boxed into an unfair pigeonhole. Instead, she's getting on with things, sometimes all at once: holding families together, holding down a job, running causes, stepping up when needed, and still — more often than not — earning less than the men beside her. She's resourceful, practical, unpretentious. She can run the sports team, the marae kitchen, the school fair — or the entire country.

Trailblazers

Kiwi women have been setting precedents for more than a century. Kate Sheppard's victory in 1893 made New Zealand the first country where women could vote.

That legacy has carried on. Helen Clark became our second female prime minister and later took a global role at the UN. Jacinda Ardern added her own stamp — empathy alongside authority — guiding the country through terrorism, a volcanic eruption, and a pandemic. Dame Silvia Cartwright broke barriers as our first female High Court judge before serving as Governor-General and later as an international judge on the Cambodian War Crimes Tribunal. Georgina Beyer redefined what leadership could look like altogether. As the world's first openly transgender mayor and later an MP, she spoke plainly about identity, justice, and dignity.

These names come up quickly when we recall our history, a sure signal to every girl growing up here that the road is open — not easy, but open.

Campaigners and Changemakers

In 1975, Dame Whina Cooper led a month-long hīkoi (march) from the Far North to Wellington, demanding that the government take "not one more acre" of Māori land. Marilyn Waring, a young National MP, boldly crossed the floor of Parliament to support the opposition Labour Party's proposed nuclear-free New Zealand policy. Louisa Wall advocated for the rights of the LGBTQI+ community. Catherine Healy, founder of the New Zealand Prostitutes' Collective, was instrumental in the campaign to decriminalise sex work.

Not all campaigners were popular in their time. Ettie Rout, during the First World War, distributed safe-sex kits to Kiwi soldiers. She was condemned by the churches and banned from being named in New Zealand newspapers, but her insistence on sexual health saved countless lives.

Leadership within te ao Māori keeps evolving too. In 2025, the new Māori Queen, Ngā wai hono i te pō Paki, took up the mantle of the Kīngitanga, urging Māori to "walk a new path".

Mana Wāhine

Leadership by wāhine Māori has shaped the nation as much as politics or sport. The kōhanga reo movement of the early 1980s, started largely by mothers and grandmothers, seeded the revival of te reo Māori. In later decades, leaders like Dame Naida Glavish, who famously defied a government order by answering phones with "Kia ora" and went on to lead major Māori health portfolios, showed that language and dignity can reshape institutions.

Traci Houpapa has become one of the country's most influential agribusiness figures as chair of the Federation of Māori Authorities, steering Māori economic development with both pragmatism and pride. Stacey Morrison, broadcaster and educator, has spent years advocating for te reo Māori in homes and schools, and Debbie Ngarewa-Packer, co-leader of Te Pāti Māori, takes mana wāhine directly into Parliament, where her speeches link whakapapa and policy.

Innovators and Creators

Culture is another place the Kiwi sheila quietly remade the landscape. Diggeress Te Kanawa revitalised the art of weaving — tukutuku and raranga — teaching and mentoring so the art was preserved and promoted. In the kitchen, Dame Alison Holst taught generations how to feed families without fuss, and her recipes are still in service. On stage and screen, Jennifer Ward-Lealand has been both artist and advocate: actor, director, champion for actors' rights, and a steady promoter of te reo Māori.

In literature, Margaret Mahy opened huge imaginative

doors for children everywhere with the 1969 publication of *A Lion in the Meadow* and went on to enchant readers with dozens of other works, full of daring plots and playful language. Alongside her, Lynley Dodd created one of our most enduring exports: *Hairy Maclary from Donaldson's Dairy* and his scruffy gang of friends, now beloved by children worldwide.

Rosemary Mount — the inventor of Kiwi Onion Dip, that pre-dinner staple built from Maggi onion soup and reduced cream — is an under-recognised icon of Kiwi cuisine. Rosemary — now in her nineties, and until recently teaching ballet to her fellow residents in a retirement village — is still determinedly modest about her contribution to New Zealand's food history.

Fashion has its sheilas as well: designers like Karen Walker and Kate Sylvester took a distinctly local sensibility offshore without pretending to be anything other than New Zealanders. Emilia Wickstead is a favourite with the Princess of Wales, and the designer of Air New Zealand's latest uniform.

And in music and faith, Shirley Erena Murray — hymn writer — gave church song around the world a distinctly Kiwi voice, with a strong thread of te reo Māori and advocacy for social justice, human rights, and ecology. Her hymns now appear in more than 140 collections worldwide, translated into numerous languages. (*Alleluia Aotearoa* remains a touchstone.)

Sport

Kiwi women have been changing the shape of sport for generations. In 1952, Dame Yvette Williams soared into history with a long jump that won New Zealand's first female Olympic gold. Forty years later, Annelise Coberger took a very different stage — the icy slopes of Albertville, France — to win silver in the slalom, the first Winter Olympic medal ever for the Southern Hemisphere.

Since then, the stories have multiplied. Dame Valerie Adams brought the shot put out of the shadows and into our living rooms, while Dame Lisa Carrington has turned canoe sprinting into one of New Zealand's surest bets at every Games. On the fairways, Lydia Ko swung her way from teen prodigy to three-time Olympic medalist and former world number one. And on the snow, Zoi Sadowski-Synnott made history in 2022 with New Zealand's first Winter Olympic gold, landing runs that seemed to bend physics as well as expectation.

Team sports have had their revolutions too. Portia Woodman-Wickliffe's lightning pace helped fill Eden Park with record crowds for women's rugby, proof that the Black Ferns could command the same stage as the All Blacks. Ameliaranne Ekenasio lifted the Silver Ferns to a World Cup and then used her captain's voice to argue for balance and well-being in professional sport. And far from the pitch, Dame Sarai Bareman, once a junior player in Auckland, now helps steer the women's game worldwide from FIFA's head office in Zurich.

Kiwi women in sport: they expand it, reshape it, and bring the crowds with them.

Work, Pay, and Power

Despite the headlines, everyday equity still wobbles. Women are the majority in health, teaching, and caring roles, but their work remains undervalued and underpaid. Flexible work is more common, yet the "double shift" of paid employment plus caregiving still falls largely on women. In the public sector, the numbers look good: women now hold more than half the board seats and close to half the chairs. Step across to the private sector, though, and the glass walls are still up: women make up only around a quarter to a third of directors and senior executives on NZX-listed companies.

There are bright spots. Teresa Gattung became the first woman to lead one of New Zealand's largest companies when she was appointed CEO of Telecom in 1999, and she later co-founded My Food Bag. More recently she launched SheEO/Coralus Aotearoa, an initiative funding women-led ventures — a deliberate shove of capital and confidence towards wāhine entrepreneurs.

Everywoman

For every headline name, there are thousands more who make a difference in quieter ways. Kiwi sheilas, often invisible, holding together families, classrooms, and communities. Their work is frequently exhausting, usually unpaid, and absolutely essential.

Sometimes, the sheila in gumboots goes global. During Cyclone Gabrielle in 2023, Kylie McIntyre, a farmer from Waipawa, called her cows as the floodwaters rose around them. All 23 animals swam more than 500 metres through swirling, muddy waters, guided only by Kylie's voice: "C'mon, c'mon, c'mon girls … *c'mon.*" The video went viral. Millions watched, astonished that a familiar call could coax an entire herd to safety.

Legends

And before all these modern names, there was Hinemoa, the young woman who, against her family's wishes, swam across Lake Rotorua to be with her lover, Tūtānekai, on Mokoia Island. The story is centuries old, but it still resonates, especially in the traditional song, "Pōkarekare Ana":

> *They are agitated, the waters of Waiapu,*
> *But when you cross over, girl, they will be calm.*
> *Oh girl, return to me, I could die of love for you.*

Determination, courage, and love strong enough to swim through the night — Hinemoa is the archetypal Kiwi sheila, the one whose example lingers in our folklore.

A Special Case: Minnie Dean

In 1895, Minnie Dean became the only woman ever executed in New Zealand, convicted of murdering infants in her care. She was a baby farmer at a time when desperate mothers had few options and social support barely existed. Whether she was a callous killer or an overwhelmed woman caught in impossible circumstances has been debated ever since. While her conviction has never been overturned, historians and legal scholars still revisit the case, asking whether public outrage and prejudice sealed her fate before the evidence was even heard.

Sheilas We're Not So Sure About

Not all Kiwi sheilas can be neatly placed on a pedestal or dismissed as villains. Some have stirred the country with political theatre, tested the law's boundaries, or taken it upon themselves to police the nation's morals. Others have lived their lives in the glare of the media, reinventing themselves while controversy trailed close behind. Their reputations remain unsettled, argued over long after the headlines have faded.

Juliet Hulme (Anne Perry)

In 1954, Juliet Hulme (15) and Pauline Parker (16) murdered Parker's mother in a Christchurch park, shocking a country that liked to think of itself as safe and respectable. Convicted of murder, both served five years in prison. Hulme left New Zealand, took the name Anne Perry, and reinvented herself as a successful writer of crime novels in Scotland. Her past caught up with her in 1994 with the release of Peter Jackson's film *Heavenly Creatures*, which dramatised the killing. For some, Perry's novels became tainted; for others, her life story underscored the disturbing thin line between imagination and reality.

Patricia Bartlett

For nearly three decades, Patricia Bartlett was the country's most determined moral campaigner. A former nun, she founded the Society for the Promotion of Community Standards in 1970 and spent the next 20 years battling "indecency" in books, magazines, television, films and advertising. Her tireless letter-writing, court submissions, and TV debates made her a household name. Admirers praised her for holding the line; detractors mocked her as joyless and censorious. In some ways, we probably needed her, but it was easier to pretend we didn't.

Lesley Martin

Lesley Martin, a former nurse from Whanganui, became the public face of the euthanasia debate after admitting she had attempted to end the suffering of her terminally ill mother in 1999. She was convicted in 2004 of attempted murder and sentenced to 15 months in prison. Before her trial she wrote *To Die Like a Dog*, a candid book arguing for compassionate law reform. Two decades on, with assisted dying now legal, her story reads as both tragic and prophetic.

Suzanne Paul

Through relentlessly cheerful infomercials — and that irritatingly unforgettable line about "thousands of luminous spheres" — Suzanne Paul became a fixture of popular culture in the 1990s. Not everything worked. Her Rawaka Māori Village tourist venture, which she described as "cabaret meets kapa haka", opened in April 2004 and was criticised by some as "tacky" or culturally questionable; it closed three months later and went into voluntary liquidation owing more than $1 million. After declaring bankruptcy in 2005, she bounced back, winning Dancing with the Stars (2007) and continuing a knack for reinvention.

Hana-Rāwhiti Kareariki Maipi-Clarke

At only 21, Hana-Rāwhiti Maipi-Clarke became the youngest MP in more than 150 years, representing Te Pāti Māori. In November 2024 she protested the Treaty Principles Bill during its first reading by ostentatiously tearing up her copy in the debating chamber and leading a haka with fellow MPs. The protest went viral, and in 2025 she was suspended from Parliament for a week. To supporters she's a bold wāhine toa; to critics, an attention-seeking provocateur.

Millie Elder-Holmes

The daughter of broadcaster Paul Holmes and psychiatrist Dr Hinemoa Elder, Millie Elder-Holmes has rarely been out of the public eye. Her struggles with addiction and a high-profile relationship with a Head Hunters gang member played out under relentless media glare. She has also shown resilience: after her father's death and the murder of her partner, she shifted into the wellness world, positioning herself as a lifestyle advocate on social media — but not above the occasional expletive. In 2025 she was fined $5,000 for promoting online gambling in breach of advertising rules, with further complaints under investigation. Some see the churn of celebrity; others, a survivor who keeps remaking herself.

So who is the Kiwi sheila?

She isn't a single figure — and that's the point. She can be prime minister or fundraiser, scientist or weaver, athlete or marae leader. She can be celebrated, controversial, or overlooked. The Kiwi bloke might come pre-packaged as a caricature. The Kiwi sheila refuses the box, and perhaps that quiet refusal is her most Kiwi quality of all.

StatChat: Life at a glance

- Life expectancy: 83.5 years overall, but it's not the same for everyone: Māori women average 77 years; Pasifika women, 78.
- Having babies later: Median age of women giving birth hit a record 31.5 in 2024.
- How many babies overall: Total fertility rate sitting around 1.56–1.60 births per woman.
- Marrying later: Median age at first marriage/civil union 30.5 in 2024.
- In the workforce: Around two-thirds of women are in paid work.
- Gender pay gap: 5.2% (median hourly, June 2025) — the lowest since records began.
- At 65, how long left: Life expectancy at 65 is 86.8 years for women (a further 21.8 years), using 2021–2023 data.
- Women in Parliament: 55 of 122 MPs as of June 2025.

HERITAGE MOMENT

The Women's Suffrage Petition, 1893

In 1893, nearly 32,000 signatures were gathered on sheets of paper pasted end to end, creating a petition 270 metres long. Women carried it through the doors of Parliament, unrolled it across the chamber floor, and demanded change. That year, New Zealand became the first country in the world to give women the vote. The petition itself survives in Archives New Zealand, its fragile pages a national taonga — the handwriting of shopgirls, teachers, housewives, widows and working women who together shifted the course of history.

Chapter Eleven

THE IGNOBLE KIWI

As Kiwis, we like to think of ourselves as reasonably good human beings. Our de facto motto could well be "Fair go, mate". But sometimes we fall short — badly, even disgracefully. A nation's identity isn't built only on pride; it's also shaped by the wounds we inflicted and the mistakes we'd rather forget.

Parihaka (1881)

On 5 November 1881, over 1,600 armed troops marched on the peaceful Taranaki settlement of Parihaka. Its leaders, Te Whiti o Rongomai and Tohu Kākahi, had chosen non-violent protest against land confiscations. They greeted the soldiers with singing children and baskets of food. The Crown's response was brutal: homes were destroyed, women were raped, and men were arrested and imprisoned without trial. Parihaka's vision of peaceful resistance was crushed, and the community left scarred. For more than a century, New Zealand governments avoided confronting this shameful invasion. In 2017, the Crown finally apologised — too late to undo the harm, but a necessary act of recognition.

The Chinese Poll Tax (1881–1944)

In 1881, New Zealand singled out Chinese migrants for a poll tax of £10 each, later raised to £100 — a huge sum at the time. No other ethnic group faced such restrictions. Shipping companies were also limited to one Chinese passenger for every 200 tons of cargo, making family reunion almost impossible. From 1908 until 1951, Chinese residents were denied the right to naturalisation, leaving many effectively shut out of full citizenship. The poll tax remained on the books until 1944, a glaring symbol of official racism. In 2002, during Chinese New Year celebrations at Parliament, Prime Minister Helen Clark delivered a formal apology, expressing "sorrow and regret that such practices were once considered appropriate". For many, the apology mattered — but it could never erase decades of exclusion.

Samoa (1918)

New Zealand administered Samoa after World War I. On 7 November 1918, officials allowed the steamer *Talune* to dock in Apia carrying passengers infected with influenza. Within weeks, the virus swept across the islands, killing more than 20 percent of the Samoan population. Families were wiped out, villages devastated, trust shattered. To Samoans, it was not a flu; it was a manmade disaster that could have been avoided. Samoans remembered the epidemic as the darkest moment of colonial rule, and bitterness lingered for generations. It was not until 2002 that New Zealand issued a formal apology for its negligence.

The Dawn Raids (1970s)

During the 1970s, Pacific Islanders were blamed for unemployment and accused of overstaying their visas. Police carried out early-morning "dawn raids", targeting Pasifika households while largely ignoring overstayers from Britain or South Africa. Families were dragged from their beds, interrogated, and deported. The raids left deep scars, feeding mistrust and humiliation that endured across generations. In 2021, Prime Minister Jacinda Ardern formally apologised to the Pasifika community for this state-sanctioned racism.

The Moyle Affair (1976)

Parliament has seen its share of rough politics, but few episodes match the cruelty of the Moyle Affair. On 6 November 1976, Prime Minister Robert Muldoon used parliamentary privilege to insinuate that police had picked up Labour MP Colin Moyle for homosexual activity. In that same session, he also referenced Moyle's alleged "effeminate giggles". In an era when homosexuality was still criminalised, the allegation was devastating. Moyle resigned, and Muldoon's attack became notorious as an abuse of power and a violation of privacy.

Erebus and the Cover-Up (1979–81)

On 28 November 1979, an Air New Zealand sightseeing flight to Antarctica slammed into the slopes of Mt Erebus, killing all 257 passengers and crew. It was New Zealand's worst peacetime disaster. The first official inquiry blamed the pilots, insisting they had flown too low. Families protested, convinced the men had been scapegoated. A Royal Commission of Inquiry, led by Justice Peter Mahon, eventually uncovered the truth: Air New Zealand had altered the flight coordinates without telling the crew, then tried to conceal the mistake. Mahon condemned the airline's actions as a "litany of lies". The attempted evasion and cover-up compounded the grief of families.

The Springbok Tour Protests (1981)

New Zealand's relationship with South Africa during the apartheid years is a shameful strand of our sporting history. As early as 1928, Māori players were excluded from All Black tours; in 1970, non-white players were grudgingly accepted only as "honorary whites". For decades, we bent our principles to keep rugby ties alive. The tensions came to a head in 1981, when the Springboks toured New Zealand. Many argued that hosting them meant condoning apartheid; others insisted politics had no place in sport. The country erupted. Protesters filled the streets, police in riot gear wielded batons, and matches were disrupted. At Hamilton, a game was abandoned after protestors stormed the field. In Auckland, flour bombs rained over Eden Park. But the deepest damage was inside homes: brothers stopped speaking, parents and children took opposite sides, neighbours turned on each other, friendships fractured. The scars lingered long after the tour was over.

Māori Loans Affair (1986–87)

The Māori Loans Affair began with an ambitious plan to raise up to NZ$600 million for Māori development through dubious intermediaries — without approval from the Minister of Finance or Cabinet. The scheme soon spiralled into chaos. When Winston Peters revealed it in Parliament on 16 December 1986, the government was stunned and the dysfunction laid bare. Senior officials resigned, and Māori leaders were left humiliated. It was not corruption in the usual sense, but a tangle of poor oversight, desperation, and mismanagement. The affair left New Zealand's credibility bruised, both at home and abroad.

Roast Busters (2013)

Not all shame comes from government. In 2013, New Zealand was rocked by the "Roast Busters" scandal, in which a group of young men in West Auckland boasted online about having sex with intoxicated underage girls. Police were criticised for failing to act despite repeated complaints. The story sparked outrage, not only at the perpetrators but also at a system that seemed unwilling to protect the vulnerable. For many, it was a sobering reflection of how ingrained misogyny and "boys will be boys" attitudes could silence victims.

Grace Millane (2018)

In December 2018, British backpacker Grace Millane was on a two-week holiday in New Zealand. When Grace failed to respond to birthday wishes her parents sent her on 2 December, police started investigating. Her body was found on 9 December. Her murder on a night when she should have been celebrating cut deep into the national conscience. New Zealanders pride themselves on being hospitable to travellers, yet here was a visitor killed within days of arriving. The day after her body was found, Prime Minister Jacinda Ardern stood in Parliament and spoke to Grace's parents: "On behalf of New Zealand," she said, "I want to apologise. Your daughter should have been safe here, and she wasn't. And I'm sorry for that."

Christchurch Mosque Shootings, 2019

On 15 March 2019, a gunman attacked two mosques in Christchurch, killing 51 people and injuring many others. It was New Zealand's darkest day in modern times, an act of terror carried out in a place that should have been safe. The horror was met with an extraordinary outpouring of compassion. Prime Minister Jacinda Ardern donned a headscarf, embraced grieving families, and declared firmly: "They are us." At vigils across the country, Kiwis stood shoulder to shoulder with the Muslim community. Out of tragedy came unity, but also an enduring sense of shame that such violence had happened here.

Embarrassments: Our Lighter Lows

Not all inglorious moments are tragic. Some are simply embarrassing — times when we made fools of ourselves in front of the world, or tripped over our own earnestness.

America's Cup "Blackheart" Campaign (2003)

When New Zealand skipper Russell Coutts defected to Swiss syndicate Alinghi in 2000, it felt like betrayal. By 2003, as Alinghi prepared to sail against Team New Zealand, the "Loyal" campaign was launched. Badges, billboards, and school projects branded Coutts a "traitor" and, most memorably, "Blackheart." The campaign whipped up hysteria: schoolchildren were encouraged to write letters denouncing him, and grown adults talked of treachery as if Coutts had defected in wartime. The spectacle made headlines overseas, and many observers cringed at how over-the-top it all looked. In the end, Alinghi beat Team New Zealand soundly, Coutts lifted the Cup for Switzerland, and our national tantrum looked faintly ridiculous. New Zealanders are known for fierce sporting loyalty, but this episode showed our thin skin when pride is pricked.

"Always Blow on the Pie" (2009)

It was supposed to be a simple public safety message. In 2009, a South Auckland police recruit video offered earnest advice about handling hot food: "Three o'clock in the morning, you're buying a pie from the BP station. What must you always do? That pie's probably been in the warming drawer for about 12 hours. It will be thermo-nuclear. You must always blow on the pie. Safer communities together, okay?" The line was deadpan, earnest, and instantly unforgettable. Within days, clips of the video were online. To this day, "Blow on the pie" remains a shorthand gag about Kiwi earnestness gone wrong.

"Nek Minnit" (2011)

In 2011, Levin skater Levi Hawken uploaded a nine-second YouTube clip. Standing in a carpark, he explained: "*Left my scooter outside the dairy. Nek minnit . . .*" The camera cut to his scooter, snapped in half. Two words became a cultural phenomenon. Within weeks, "*Nek minnit*" was voted runner-up in a "Word of the Year" poll in 2011. At first, we laughed at the randomness. Then came a pang of remorse. Hawken, with his unusual appearance caused by a rare genetic condition, became the butt of the joke as much as the clip itself. Shamefully, our instinct had been to laugh first and reflect later.

David Cunliffe's "I'm Sorry for Being a Man" (2014)

On 4 July 2014, Labour leader David Cunliffe stood at a women's refuge forum to launch his party's domestic violence policy. He chose to begin with an apology: "Can I begin by saying I'm sorry. I don't often say it. I'm sorry for being a man, because family and sexual violence is overwhelmingly perpetrated by men." His intention was clear: to acknowledge male responsibility and show solidarity with women. But the line was instantly ridiculed; critics gleefully portrayed him as weak and self-flagellating. Even some supporters winced, wishing he had found better words. The phrase "sorry for being a man" overshadowed the policy itself and became one of the defining images of his short, troubled leadership.

The Flag Referendum (2015–16)

In 2015, John Key's government invited New Zealanders to decide whether it was time to ditch the old Union Jack-stamped flag for something fresh. The process cost more than $26 million, included a nationwide design competition, and stirred a torrent of ridicule. Public submissions produced outlandish entries, the most famous being "Laser Kiwi" — a green bird shooting a red laser beam from its eyes. While the finalists were more conventional, many voters dismissed the whole exercise as a vanity project. In 2016, after two referenda, the verdict was clear: the old flag stayed. Some claimed the money could have been better spent on hospitals or schools; others grumbled about being asked to choose at all. The flag referendum turned out to be a costly debate that produced no change. The only real winner was Laser Kiwi.

The Waitangi Dildo Incident (2016)

On 5 February 2016, the day before Waitangi Day, Economic Development Minister Steven Joyce was fronting media at Te Tii Marae when a protester launched a sex toy at his face. The projectile — a large pink dildo — smacked him squarely, bouncing harmlessly away. Joyce barely flinched, quipping "Good-oh" as cameras rolled. The images rocketed around the world within hours. International headlines dubbed it "Dildogate", and social media christened Joyce "Dildo Baggins". The nation cringed, Joyce wore it with humour, the protester made her point, and the rest of us were left shaking our heads of the absurdity of it all.

HERITAGE MOMENT

Farid forgives

At the national remembrance service in Hagley Park on 29 March 2019, the crowd of 20,000 listened as Christchurch community member Farid Ahmed took the stage. Two weeks earlier, his wife Husna had been killed while helping others escape the Al Noor mosque shootings. Ahmed, a wheelchair user since a car accident years before, had remained at home that day.

Now, facing a grieving nation, he spoke with calm conviction. "I don't want a heart that is boiling like a volcano," he said. "I want a heart that is full of love and care. And I forgive him." Silence fell across the park. People wept, clasped hands, and bowed their heads, moved by the extraordinary grace of a man choosing compassion over hatred.

Chapter Twelve

KIWI NUTS AND BOLTS

"New Zealand is not a small country, but a large village."

—PETER JACKSON

Getting Around: Driving and Transport

Drive on the left, give way to the right, and always wear a seatbelt. These are the written rules. What's less often mentioned is that you should also keep left on a footpath (and on escalators), and if a police officer tells you to pull over because of a driving offence, stay in your car.

A quick thank-you wave is standard when someone lets you into a queue of traffic or stops for you at a pedestrian crossing.

Road rage does happen, but Kiwis are usually convinced they're excellent drivers, and that it's "every other idiot on the road" who's responsible for any near misses. If you make a mistake, don't be surprised to receive a one-finger salute — a universally recognisable signal of disapproval.

Most city centres have limited free parking. Many Kiwis curse parking wardens and tow-truck drivers — often with feeling, and sometimes with good reason.

Freedom camping and long road trips are part of the culture, and campervan drivers often greet each other like old friends.

SMART MOVE: Download Transit or Moovit to navigate regional public transport with ease.

Local Knowledge: Going on a "tiki tour" means taking the unnecessarily long way from Point A to Point B. Unscrupulous taxi drivers might try to take tourists on a tiki tour between the airport and their hotel to earn a better fare.

Healthcare and Emergencies

- Many Kiwis take a "she'll be right" approach to injuries and illnesses — they won't rush to A&E unless it's serious.
- GPs are usually on a first-name basis with patients; formal titles aren't common.
- Pharmacies double as mini health hubs, offering quick medical advice, free checks, and vaccinations for Covid or the flu.
- Around 40% of hospital nurses trained overseas — a reminder that New Zealand's healthcare system depends on its diverse migrant workforce.
- Tune in to Newstalk ZB at 11:00 pm on Sundays for The Nutters Club, two hours of raw interviews and discussions on mental health. It's a Kiwi favourite for tackling the tough stuff people often avoid talking about.

SMART MOVE: Become a member of Hato Hone St John for reduced-cost emergency ambulance services, 24/7, 365 days a year. Explore more of their medical services at stjohn.org.nz.

LOCAL KNOWLEDGE: Kiwi blokes have a reputation for being slow to discuss their health — physical or mental — even with their mates. "Movember" (moustache + November) is when many men grow a mo' to raise awareness and funds for men's health. It started in Australia, but Kiwis

MOVEMBER

embraced it wholeheartedly — our blokes need all the help they can get.

Education: Schools and Learning the Ropes

- State schools request "voluntary" donations to cover tuition fees. Fundraising events are woven into school life: sausage sizzles, raffles, quiz nights. Participation and volunteering are noticed — and appreciated.
- Don't be surprised if you hear teachers (and often principals) addressed by first names.
- Kids might go barefoot at school and on the sports field and nobody bats an eyelid.
- Shortcomings with assessment systems like NCEA (National Certificate of Educational Achievement) have been recognised by the Ministry of Education, and changes are in progress. Increasing numbers of schools offer Cambridge exams or the International Baccalaureate as an alternative to NCEA.
- Communication from schools to parents is app-based and informal. Expect push notifications rather than paper notes in schoolbags.

SMART MOVE: Download the school's app (Hero, Skool Loop, Seesaw) early. It's where everything happens.

LOCAL KNOWLEDGE: The perception of "good school zones" still drives house prices.

Money, Banking and Shopping

- Eftpos is king, even for a $6 flat white or other small purchases. Many Kiwis rarely carry cash.
- Although a tip jar may sit quietly by the till, tipping isn't a given. The danger is that wait-staff will sometimes give better service to a guest they think will tip generously and neglect other tables.
- Op shops (charity shops) and second-hand buying are not just accepted, they're often admired as thrifty and eco-friendly.
- Weekend farmers' markets are as much about community and a chat as they are about shopping.
- Everyone knows cash jobs are a form of tax evasion, but many Kiwis still ask tradespeople (especially in construction) about informal deals — known as "mate's rates".

SMART MOVE: Check Trade Me and Facebook Marketplace for bargains. Op shops are everywhere and firmly mainstream.

LOCAL KNOWLEDGE: Pak'nSave = cheapest, Woolworths = mid-range, New World = the "fancy" option. The Warehouse: "Where everyone gets a bargain!"

Work and Employment

- There are about 612,000 registered businesses in Aotearoa. A staggering 97% are small businesses with fewer than 20 employees.
- First names are standard, even for CEOs.
- Expect an informal culture: shared lunches are common, and Friday after-work drinks happen in many workplaces. Taking turns to "shout" (pay for a round of drinks for everyone in your group) is appreciated. Don't skip your turn.
- The gender pay gap is real. Latest figures show that for every dollar a man earns, a woman earns approximately 92 cents.
- Work-life balance matters; working late isn't a badge of honour. However, bosses will take a dim view of anyone "taking a sickie" (calling in sick when they're not actually unwell).

SMART MOVE: The Citizens Advice Bureau (CAB) provides free, practical help with contracts, pay rights, and CVs.

LOCAL KNOWLEDGE: Most employees get four weeks of paid annual leave each year, plus public holidays. Many workplaces also shut down over Christmas–New Year, so staff are expected to save some of their leave for that break.

Social Norms

- Many public events begin with a karakia (a Māori blessing). Stand or sit respectfully.
- Small talk avoids politics, religion, and money at a first

meeting. Weather, sport, and roadworks are always safe topics.

- If you're invited to someone's home, it's normal to take a bottle of wine or some flowers as a gift.
- Acknowledging and thanking service staff is standard. We're not fond of people who think they're better than others. Call out a friendly "Thank you, driver!" as you get off the bus.
- Turning up unannounced at someone's home isn't popular. But a quick call or text — "Are you up for a visit tomorrow? I can bring lunch" — will almost always get you invited over.

SMART MOVE: When you're invited to someone's home, ask as you arrive if they'd like you to remove your shoes.

LOCAL KNOWLEDGE: Personal space matters. In most social interactions, keep roughly an arm's length from others. With friends or family, it may be less, but an arm's length is common. And always try to make eye contact when talking. It shows you're engaged and respectful.

Sustainability and the Environment

- Recycling correctness — separating waste into the right categories for recycling and disposal — is a weekly ritual. Tossing your excess rubbish into someone else's wheelie bin (usually under cover of darkness) is a no-no. Neighbours notice.
- Although city councils run intermittent inorganic collections, it's common to see an informal system of recycling in action — unwanted furniture and other

usable household items left on the footpath, free to anyone who wants to collect them.

- Single-use plastic shopping bags are gone, and most people support the ban by taking their own bags to the supermarket.
- Composting and worm farms are practically suburban status symbols.
- Tramping etiquette (Leave No Trace) is taken seriously. Locals will call out bad behaviour.

SMART MOVE: Share a meal that makes a difference: visit or support Everybody Eats in Onehunga or Glen Innes (in Auckland), or Wellington. This "pay as you feel" restaurant turns surplus food into great dinners for people facing food insecurity.

LOCAL KNOWLEDGE: You'll see "little free libraries" dotted around Kiwi suburbs — small roadside boxes where you can take a book and leave a book. They're a low-key example of our reuse culture.

Where to Go for Help

- Citizens Advice Bureau (CAB): www.cab.org.nz
- New Zealand Now (Government info for migrants): www.newzealandnow.govt.nz
- Immigration NZ: www.immigration.govt.nz
- Tenancy Services: www.tenancy.govt.nz
- IRD (tax): www.ird.govt.nz
- Health Navigator NZ: www.healthnavigator.org.nz

At a Glance: Emergency Phone Numbers

- Life-threatening — 111 (Police, Ambulance, Fire)
- Medical advice — 0800 611 116 (Healthline)
- Mental health — 1737 (Need to Talk?)
- AA Roadservice — 0800 500 222
- Poison emergency — 0800 764 766 (Poisons Centre)

The Kiwi Iconic Alphabet

A is for Aroha

More than just "love," aroha in te ao Māori also means compassion, empathy, and deep connection. "Arohanui" means "with deep respect".

B is for Buzzy Bee

This brightly painted wooden pull-along toy has been clattering across Kiwi floors since the 1940s. The Buzzy Bee made international headlines when Prince William played with one during a royal visit in 1983.

C is for Coffee Culture

Flat white, trim latte, oat milk cappuccino? Even the smallest town has a decent espresso machine and a barista with opinions. Kiwi café culture is strong — and proudly filter-free.

D is for Dairy

Not the cows — the corner shop. Stocked with snacks, basic groceries, milk, loo paper, ice creams, and a bit of neighbourhood chat. You can probably even buy your weekly Lotto ticket there.

E is for *Edmonds Cookery Book*

With over 3.45 million copies sold since it was first published in 1908, Edmonds is New Zealand's culinary bible. Still referred to when recipes for classic Kiwi culinary stalwarts are called for.

F is for Fish and Chips

A Friday night classic, best eaten on the beach or in your lap. Snapper takes the prize for the best variety of fish, but terakihi, gurnard and hoki are also good. Try a paua fritter or a battered mussel or two while you're at it.

G is for Gumboots

Essential rural footwear and a national icon. Honoured in song by comic character Fred Dagg and celebrated in Taihape's gumboot-throwing festival. If you've never owned a pair, are you even Kiwi?

H is for Heitiki

Not just a souvenir, the greenstone tiki pendant is a sacred Māori taonga. Once given out in plastic form by the national airline, it's now worn with pride, meaning, and mana.

I is for Interislander

The ferry trip between the North and South Islands is stunning on a good day and soul-testing on a bad one. Either way, it's an unforgettable part of the Kiwi journey. The 92km voyage takes 3 hours.

J is for Jandals

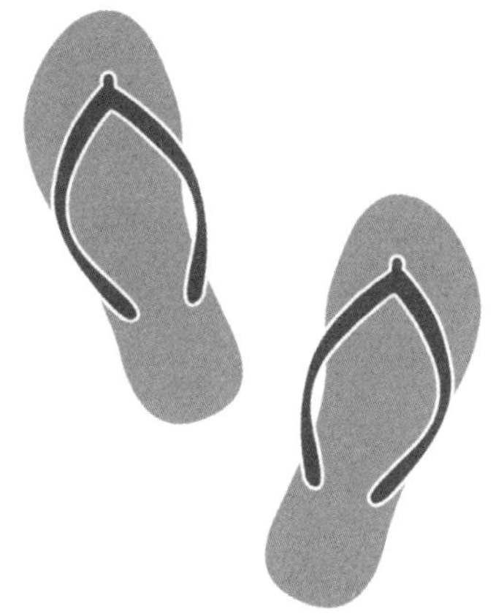

The country's surf lifesavers run an annual fundraising appeal in December called National Jandal Day, when everyone is encouraged to wear their jandals and donate generously to help lifesavers save lives on New Zealand's beaches.

K is for Kōrero

To kōrero is to speak, share, and connect. From a yarn with a stranger to a formal welcome on a marae, kōrero is at the heart of Kiwi life and a respected way of solving disputes.

L is for Lotto

Every Saturday night we watch the bouncing balls and dream big. Most of us won't win — but someone always does, and that's reason enough to buy a ticket.

M is for Marmite

Saltier and darker than its Aussie cousin called Vegemite, Marmite has been a Kiwi favourite since 1919. When factory damage caused a national shortage in 2012, we called it "Marmageddon".

N is for Nuclear-Free Zone

On 10 July 1985, the Greenpeace protest ship *Rainbow Warrior* was blown up in the Auckland harbour by two French secret agents. Their terrorist action cemented in us a very determined anti-nuclear stance that would be enshrined in Nuclear Free Zone legislation within two years. We still stand by it.

O is for Opo

In the summer of 1955, a friendly dolphin started playing in the surf at Opononi. She let children swim with her, followed boats, and captured the nation's heart. A statue still stands in her honour.

P is for Pōwhiri

The formal welcome ceremony on a marae is full of ritual, language, waiata and respect. It can be emotional, spine-tingling, and unforgettable — a powerful experience for those invited in.

Q is for Queen Street

Auckland's busiest street has seen it all — student protests, Santa parades, buskers, tourists, office workers, late-night snacks and early-morning regrets. Unfortunately, it's also where the unwary driver is likely to cop a $150 fine for accidentally turning into a bus lane. With its ever-shifting road cones, safety fencing, one-way traps and cryptic signage, Queen Street has become something of a fundraising tool for Auckland Transport. Proceed — with caution.

R is for Rugby

Game, obsession, religion. Learn the rules, pick a team, and never underestimate how much a single All Blacks win (or loss) can affect the national mood.

S is for Shrek

Among the national flock of 31 million, we found a

celebrity — a merino sheep who avoided being shorn for six years and became a global star. His 27 kg fleece was removed on live TV. He toured the country, met the PM, and raised $150,000 for charity. He died a hero at the age of 17.

T is for Tui Billboards

Cheeky and controversial, Tui's "Yeah, right" billboards poked fun at politics, pop culture, and Kiwi life. For example, just before Waitangi Day 2008, Tui erected a billboard that said "Muskets, blankets and beads. Sounds like a fair trade . . . Yeah, right." Still iconic.

U is for UV

New Zealand sunshine burns fast and fierce, and our melanoma rates are high. Sunscreen isn't optional — it's armour. Each summer the nationwide SunSmart programme tells us to "Slip, Slop, Slap and Wrap": slip on a shirt, slop on the 30+ sunscreen, slap on a hat, and wear wraparound sunglasses.

V is for Villa

Once humble wooden homes, now real estate gold. Think tin roofs, sash windows, and kauri floorboards — the classic Kiwi villa is charm with a price tag.

W is for Wētā

The wētā is a terrifyingly large, biting insect with spiny hind legs, native to New Zealand. An adult wētā weighs around 70 g. Wētā is also the name of the creative workshop based in Wellington that made the models and designed the special effects in many of Peter Jackson's movie masterpieces, such as *The Hobbit* and *Lord of the Rings*.

X is for X-treme Sports

We like our adventures bold: bungy jumping, white-water rafting, skydiving — the more terrifying, the better. Queenstown turned adrenaline into an artform. Thrill-seeking is practically a local sport.

Y is for "Yeah, nah"

A brilliantly succinct and soothingly noncommittal Kiwi way of saying that you have heard what another person has said, and you might agree — but then again you might not. Once you've mastered it, you're halfway to fluent.

Z is for Zorbing

Invented in Rotorua, the Zorb is a large transparent sphere with another slightly smaller one inside it. You climb into the inner sphere and roll down a slope at great speed. Ridiculous? Definitely. But also kind of genius.

Chapter Thirteen

KIWI OCCASIONS

Glance quickly at a diary of a year in the life of Aotearoa and you risk exhaustion. It looks as though the whole nation is off exerting themselves in strenuous sports year-round. But there are also foodie adventures to sample, artistic triumphs to admire, and sombre historical moments to reflect on. One thing's certain: there's no excuse to feel bored.

JANUARY

Sun-soaked holidays stretch on. City offices are quiet, motorways unclogged, and beach towns humming. It's hot in the north, warm and bright in the south, with long golden evenings and the smell of barbecues drifting on the breeze. Now and then, a cyclone sweeps down from the Pacific and turns campgrounds into lagoons.

Auckland Anniversary Regatta

Held every year except one since 1850, this is thought to be the world's largest one-day regatta. Waitematā Harbour fills with tall ships, sloops, multihulls, dragonboats, powerboats, vintage tugs, yachts and Māori waka. Find a perch on North Head or along Tāmaki Drive and watch the whole watery circus glide by.

ASB Classic

A compact, intimate tennis tournament where you're so close to the action you can practically hear players muttering at themselves. The women's and men's weeks take up the first two weeks of January and attract big names warming up for the Australian Open later in the month.

Karaka Million

The richest night in New Zealand racing. Under Ellerslie's

floodlights, thoroughbreds fly and fascinators bloom on the eve of the National Yearling Sales. International buyers, owners and trainers size up future champions. The racing is fast, the stakes are high, and the crowd dresses for the occasion.

FEBRUARY

Back-to-school reality bites, but February has other ideas. Global climate change has nudged the seasons forward by about a month. The days are hot, the evenings still stretch out, and half the country wonders if the school holidays are mistimed.

Waitangi Day — 6 February

Each year on 6 February, Aotearoa pauses for a day that is part celebration, part soul-searching. Ceremonies are held around the country, the most prominent at the Waitangi Treaty Grounds in the Bay of Islands. Crowds gather on the marae and waterfront as waka glide across the harbour, kapa haka groups perform, and the national flag is raised to the sound of conch shells and karanga. It became a nationwide public holiday in 1974, after Prime Minister Norman Kirk introduced the legislation. Since then, prime ministers have come expecting both ceremony and challenge, and are met with everything from respectful greetings to heckling and protest placards. For many, the day is a reminder of the work still to be done. For most, it's simply nice to have another holiday.

Kathmandu Coast to Coast

A two-day gut-buster of a challenge from Kumara on the West Coast to New Brighton Beach in Christchurch: a full 243 km of cycling, running (most of it over the Southern Alps), then kayaking through the Waimakariri Gorge. Brutal.

Mission Estate Concert

Each summer, Mission Estate Winery becomes a natural amphitheatre as thousands picnic on the lawns under the Hawke's Bay sun. Past headliners have included opera star Kiri Te Kanawa, Elton John, Rod Stewart, Stevie Nicks, Sting, and Robbie Williams.

MARCH

March brings long, calm days and golden light. The sun still has generous warmth, the beaches are still busy, and most of the country is quietly glad summer seems in no hurry to leave — though evenings turn cooler a little sooner in the South Island.

Pasifika Festival

Western Springs Park in Auckland becomes a two-day constellation of Pacific "villages" with captivating music, dancing, drumming, craft and food from eleven island communities. One of Auckland's happiest weekends.

Hokitika Wildfoods Festival

Whitebait patties and wild pork sausages for the sensible; chocolate-coated huhu grubs and sheep's testicles for the brave. The wasp-larvae ice cream is supposed to be good, too. If your appetite falters, the scenery won't.

Golden Shears (Masterton)

The world's most famous shearing and wool-handling championships. Watch a champion drag out a sheep, flip it on its back and deftly shear off a fleece in seconds — without nicking the wool, the sheep or themselves.

Gumboot Throwing Championships (Taihape)

Of course gumboot throwing is a sport! Kids, grandparents, and serious contenders all have a go. The rules are simple: the winner is whoever hurls a boot farthest.

APRIL

Crisp mornings, mellow afternoons. Easter brings traffic jams and chocolate. Down south, a few inland fields might wake up wearing a thin frost — just enough to make everyone check their firewood supply or wonder how much longer they can get away without turning the heat pump on.

Running of the Sheep (Te Kūiti)

On the final day of the Great NZ Muster, Te Kūiti's main streets will be closed to traffic while over 1,000 Romney sheep thunder down the main street in a woolly version of Pamplona's Running of the Bulls. A prize is given for correctly guessing the number of sheep.

Warbirds Over Wanaka (biennial, Easter)

Historic fighter planes roar overhead, contemporary jets scream past, and grown men get something in their eye. The show ends with a staged "air battle" complete with pyrotechnics.

Anzac Day — 25 April

Before dawn on 25 April 1915, New Zealand and Australian troops landed on Turkey's Gallipoli Peninsula. Poor planning, steep cliffs and determined resistance turned the campaign into a tragedy. More than 130,000 soldiers died, including 2,799 New Zealanders. Out of the mud and chaos, something else formed: identity. New Zealanders began to see themselves as distinct — tested by hardship, bound by mateship, and capable of courage under impossible conditions.

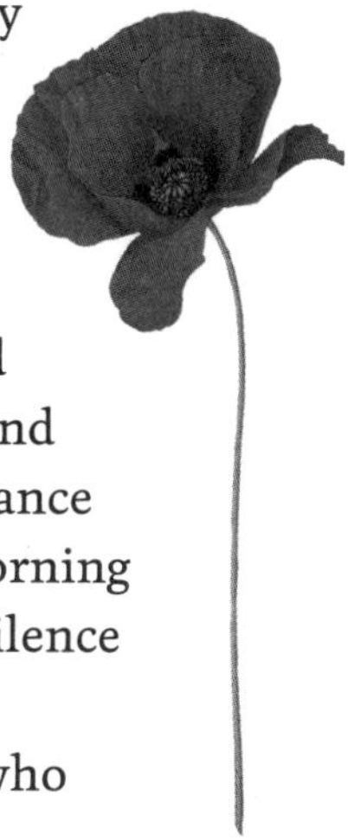

Today, crowds gather in the half-light for dawn services from Kaitaia to Bluff. The bugle sounds the Last Post; poppies are pinned to lapels; wreaths are laid beneath cenotaphs and memorial gates. We hear the Ode of Remembrance — "At the going down of the sun and in the morning / We will remember them" — then stand in a silence that feels deeper than the hour.

The day has evolved. It still honours those who served and died, but it has widened to include veterans of later conflicts, peacekeepers, and families who carry the weight of war. Children place small wooden crosses; former refugees bow their heads beside fourth-generation farmers; RSA clubs open their doors.

MAY

Autumn deepens. Central Otago blazes gold and orange while Aucklanders dig out jumpers and pretend it's cold. The days grow shorter, the evenings draw in, and life shifts indoors ... but the calendar stays lively enough to keep winter from creeping fully into the national mood just yet.

Bluff Oyster Festival

The season's first Bluffies are celebrated with shucking and eating contests, live music and a heroic 30,000 oysters consumed in one day.

Firefighter Sky Tower Stair Challenge (Auckland)

Around 500 firefighters, in full gear with 25 kg of breathing apparatus, charge up 51 flights (1,103 steps) of the Sky Tower to raise funds for Leukaemia & Blood Cancer NZ.

New Zealand Gold Guitar Awards (Gore)

It's all banjos, steel guitars and fiddles (and, undoubtedly, cowboy boots) for a week of country music. Gore's answer to Nashville stages competitions, concerts and inductions into its local "Hands of Fame".

JUNE

The shortest days arrive. Snow settles on the mountain tops (not so much at low levels yet), southerlies blow up from Antarctica, and everyone debates when to surrender and turn on the heat pump. Morning commutes are darker now, and the country feels ready for soup, slippers and rugby.

No. 8 Wire National Art Award (Hamilton)

Kiwi ingenuity turned into sculpture, all created from the humble fencing wire that once fixed just about everything.

Fieldays (Mystery Creek, Waikato)

The Southern Hemisphere's largest agricultural event: four days of innovation, giant machinery, gumboots and good deals on ride-on mowers.

JULY

Midwinter. North Island cities turn grey and drizzly, while the South Island often wakes to hard frosts, blue skies and snow-bright mountains. Fresh dumps of snow blanket the ski fields, and on clear days the cold air sparkles.

Matariki — Māori New Year

Matariki is the name given to a cluster of stars (known elsewhere as the Pleiades) whose reappearance in the pre-dawn sky signals Māori New Year. It usually rises in midwinter, a natural pause between harvest and planting. For many iwi, Matariki carries three intertwined strands: remembering those who have died, celebrating the present, and planning for the future.

The names of the stars hint at their roles. Tupuānuku and Tupuārangi are linked to food from the earth and sky; Waitī and Waitā to waters fresh and salt; Waipunarangi to rain; Ururangi to winds. Pōhutukawa is associated with remembrance — the loved ones who have passed in the year just gone. Hiwa-i-te-rangi looks forward, a star of aspirations and wishes for the year ahead.

Communities mark Matariki in different ways. Some host hautapu ceremonies at dawn, offering the steam of cooked food to the stars. Others hold night markets, storytelling sessions, kapa haka and kai. Families gather to share memories and set intentions. Since becoming a public holiday in 2022, Matariki has grown into a rare thing: a home-grown national celebration that invites all of us — newcomers and old hands — to pause, remember, and reset together.

FMG Young Farmer of the Year (Grand Final)

Practical skills meet business smarts: finalists shear sheep, fix fences, balance budgets and front the media.

AUGUST

Frosty mornings, bright afternoons. Daffodils poke through, and the first lambs totter across the paddocks. Everyone's quietly over winter, but winter isn't done with us. Icy winds can still howl through, but with a few layers of merino clothing on our own bodies, the sight of new life makes the chill easier to shrug off.

Phantom Billstickers National Poetry Day
Words pop up everywhere: buses, pubs, bookshops and community halls. Readings, open-mics and the odd poem chalked on the pavement.

Bledisloe Cup (All Blacks v Wallabies)
The All Blacks and Australia square off each year, typically over two Tests in late winter/early spring. We've had the cup parked on the mantelpiece since 2003 — but we still watch it like a hawk.

Winter Games NZ (Queenstown/Wānaka/Naseby)
Elite skiers, snowboarders and curlers bring a burst of Olympic-level sparkle to the deep south.

SEPTEMBER
Spring sidles in — or so the calendar claims. We're not sure whether it starts on the first of the month or we should wait for the equinox. In any case, the daytime weather is irritatingly fickle. The nights still call for heaters and a decent duvet.

WOW/World of WearableArt (Wellington)
Part catwalk, part theatre, part fever dream. Sculptural garments come alive on stage in a riot of colour, light and choreography.

Wayleggo Cup (Trans-Tasman Sheepdog Trials)

Held alternately in New Zealand and Australia, with dogs working gates, ramps and a Maltese cross on a timed course — proof that Kiwi genius often has four legs and a tail.

OCTOBER

The clocks jump forward, lawns seem to sprout overnight, and the whole country starts to twitch. Exams loom, the first spring weddings are celebrated, and hay fever launches its annual attack. Energy levels rise with the daylight hours, and people begin plotting summer trips and projects.

Armageddon Expo (Auckland, Labour Weekend)

Gaming, comics, collectibles, cosplay and committed nerd-joy. Families, teens and nostalgic forty-somethings all find their tribe.

Labour Day — The Eight-Hour Day

In 1840, a carpenter named Samuel Parnell reportedly told a prospective employer in Wellington he would work only eight hours a day: "There are twenty-four hours in a day — eight for work, eight for sleep, and eight for recreation." Others followed his lead, and by the late nineteenth century, union campaigns had turned an idea into a movement. In 1890, huge Labour Day parades rolled through the main centres behind banners demanding fair hours and fair pay.

The public holiday we enjoy today (the fourth Monday in October) carries that history inside it. Shops no longer shut for massive processions, but the principle remains: life is bigger than work. For many New Zealanders it's the first proper spring long weekend — a chance to plant tomatoes, dig out the tent, or simply lie under a tree and do nothing at all. Work-life balance is a modern phrase, but the instinct behind it is old and stubbornly Kiwi: everyone deserves a fair go and a bit of time off.

NOVEMBER

Hay bales dot the paddocks, pōhutukawa buds swell, and the days stretch long again. The country's energy lifts, even as the first Christmas ads appear on TV, to most people's dismay. Traffic thickens, school terms end, and summer holidays begin to glimmer just ahead on the horizon.

Lake Taupō Cycle Challenge

New Zealand's biggest bike event sends thousands of riders around a 160 km loop. The front of the field is fast; the back of the field is happy; everyone sleeps well.

Canterbury A&P Show (Christchurch)

Three days of rural pride: cattle groomed to a shine, horses plaited and prancing, woodchopping, shearing and the grand parade.

Toast Martinborough

A progressive wine festival where ticketholders wander between boutique vineyards sipping pinot and nibbling gourmet snacks under the spring sun.

Farmers Santa Parade (Auckland)

Floats, bands and superheroes stream through the CBD until Santa waves from his sleigh in full red regalia under a sky that's far too warm for fur-trimmed hats.

DECEMBER

Long bright evenings, crowded beaches and the hum of lawnmowers. Schools wind down for the year, office parties reach full swing, and Christmas shopping chaos clogs the malls. Out-of-office replies get switched on, camping gear comes out of sheds, and the whole country winds down — usually near a barbecue.

Coca-Cola Christmas in the Park

Families spread blankets in the Auckland Domain and Christchurch's Hagley Park for an evening of live music and fireworks, with donations supporting Surf Life Saving New Zealand.

Rhythm and Vines (Gisborne)

An end-of-year music festival set among vines at Waiohika Estate — first in the world to see the new year dawn.

TIP: Event dates and venues can shift year to year (or every second year), so check the current listings before you go. But the spirit of each occasion — the thing that makes it "us" — is steady as a rock.

Chapter Fourteen

A KIWI KIND OF LIFE

There's no single Kiwi life story — our ethnic spread puts paid to that — and no rulebook about what to do when, but if you squint, you might just see a familiar pattern.

Early childhood (0–4): First steps

- Days at playgroup or daycare, learning to share toys while your mums (or dads) commiserate over coffee.
- Playdates, playgrounds, picture books and paint-smeared art smocks.
- Learning to count, wait your turn, and say goodbye at the daycare gate without tears (most days).
- Watching older siblings disappear into the mysterious world of school, and counting down the days until it's your turn.

Primary years (5–12): Learning the ropes

- Shoes on (mostly), phones away for the school day.
- Singing "God Defend New Zealand" in te reo at school assemblies.
- Kapa haka practice, sausage sizzles and the occasional mufti (no-uniform) day.
- Family trips to the bach (or crib) where you keep asking "Are we there yet?"

- Saturday morning sport: ripper rugby, football, netball, and fluoro mouthguards lost in the grass.

Teens (13–19): The stretch years

- The first school ball outfit that will haunt your photo albums forever.
- Leadership camps, the Duke of Edinburgh's Award, school productions, or the first part-time job stacking shelves.
- Worrying about having to be an adult one day; careers days at school.
- Learning to drive — parallel parks on hills, handbrakes at the ready — and counting down to that restricted licence at 16½.
- A deeper encounter with te ao Māori through kapa haka, waiata, or visits to a marae.
- Finding your crew through sport, music, gaming or activism — while navigating social media and the quiet pull of vapes despite the health warnings.

Twenties: The big leap

- Tertiary study or straight to work; flatting with people you'll be friends with forever — or won't speak to again (and plenty staying home longer to save).
- Your OE (Overseas Experience) if the budget allows — a rite of passage that has taken generations to London pubs, Canadian ski fields, and beyond.
- Coming home with a better appreciation for Mum's roast dinners and laundry skills — and maybe even Dad's jokes.
- The first serious go at a career, the first serious go at a relationship, and the first serious talk about whether to buy a house in a market that always seems to be getting away from you.

Thirties: Anchoring

- Careers deepen; some switch tracks entirely.
- Partnerships become marriages or civil unions — or amicable "we're better as friends" realignments.
- Babies for some; dogs for others; proud plant parents for the rest.
- Hoping that the Bank of Mum and Dad is still open to lending you money for your first home, perhaps a townhouse rather than the old quarter-acre. Renovations become a weekend hobby and a money pit.
- A growing instinct to volunteer: coaching a kids' team, serving on a school board, joining in beach clean-ups.

Forties: Full tilt

- Juggling growing kids, ageing parents, and work.
- Discovering that book clubs are for people like you, not just nerds.
- Taking real holidays in your own country and wondering why you spent your OE in drizzly flats when Queenstown exists.
- A second wave of study for some — MBAs, teaching, nursing, tradie retraining, or creative writing courses that finally get that novel moving.

Fifties: Changing gears

- Downsizing or sea-changing; joining the local choir, tramping club, or men's/women's shed.
- Becoming deeply knowledgeable about native birds at the feeder or native plants in the garden. Finding the time to grow your own vegetables.
- Grandparent energy (for some): ferrying kids to sport, refusing to accept thanks for home baking.

- A quiet pride in (and a few worries about) seeing the next generation "give it a go" in their own way.

Sixties: Not done yet

- Planning for retirement ... but quietly carrying on. About one in four New Zealanders aged 65+ are still in paid work.
- Balancing paid work with volunteering, hobbies and travel. Group travel and European river cruises seem more desirable than trekking through Bhutan.
- More time for friends, grandchildren, film festivals and long lunches (often midweek, just because you can).

Seventies and eighties: Letting go (a bit)

- Stepping back from paid work — or finally retiring completely.
- Moving closer to family, or into smaller homes that don't need constant upkeep.
- Starting to disburse family heirlooms and decluttering your living space.
- Considering the lifestyle, security and company of a retirement village.
- Wondering if it's time to record your family history.

AFTERWORD

Back in that hotel bar, the question was, "So, where on earth is New Zealand, anyway?"

After these pages, you know the answer. It isn't just 41° South, 174° East. **It's here.** It's the place where dawn breaks first, where we make fun of ourselves as easily as we celebrate our heroes, where welcome and joining in matter more than polish or perfection.

It's the place where neighbours leave help-yourself boxes of feijoas on the berm, communities rally after cyclones, and world-class athletes still head home after the competition. It's where te reo Māori is heard more often in classrooms, workplaces and Parliament, and where we're learning — slowly but surely — to celebrate both our roots and our differences.

It's the place where a flat white still fuels half the nation, and a supermarket onion dip has somehow become part of the national DNA. It's the place where Saturday mornings are for netball courts and rugby fields, Sunday mornings for the farmers' market, and where silence under a night sky full of stars can hush even the chattiest Kiwi. It's where people stumble, and forgive, and try again. It's where we hope to be small but never small-minded, remote but never out of reach.

It's where, at the end of a long day, we'll still tell you: this is the centre of the bloody universe.

The kettle's on. Haere mai.